MUSES OF A
RESTLESS MIND

Norman Rivera Gonzalez

Inquiries & Contact Information:

nrgwriting@gmail.com

Facebook: NRG Writing

TABLE OF CONTENTS

ACKNOWLEDGEMENTS

I would like to thank all of my friends, family, fellow authors and colleagues for your kind and patient support in writing this book.

Rose Rivera, for helping me get this book together to its final stage of publishing. Your keen insight has been appreciated and kind.

Nilda Velez, my sincere thanks who pushed me to write as she wanted to add this book to her collection of my writing.

Giuseppe Bonnano, my best friend who is like a brother. Thank you!

Nelson Lopez, my great friend. for encouraging me to write and put the magical words on paper.

My audience in my Face Book forum, NRG Writing, that enjoy my writing and keep asking me for more. Your appreciation is heartfelt by me.

Palmira Gonzalez, my mother, thank you! Your support and love with my zaniness, especially when I was writing in the wee hours of the morning or late at night. I love you immensely for being my rock.

I cannot forget to thank the fans of my two previously published books "Diary of a Mad Hatter" and "Darkness and Lightness".

My heartfelt thanks to all.

INTRODUCTION

I'm sharing my innermost thoughts and creative writing with you in this book, "Muses of a Restless Mind".

My inspiration in the prose and poems have been humankind and nature.

Daily conversations and encounters with folks I admire and love.

Some of the writing is uplifting and others slightly sad.

My intentions in my writing is to let you know, that you are not alone.

Many of the characters you will "meet" in my writing, you will recognize as yourself or other people that you may know.

My wish is for you to enjoy my writing, that it pulls you, touch the depths of your soul and mind, and makes sense to your past and current being.

I promise you, there is something for everyone in this book,

Enjoy!

Norman Rivera Gonzalez

9-1-1

She went to bed at nine thirty at night, unusually early for her.

She was sleepy.

Complaining of dizziness and chest pain as well.

Her son, who loved her dearly, tucked her into bed and bade her good night.

He decided to call it an early night as well and went to bed, although not very sleepy.

Two hours into the night, her son, heard her yell, calling him.

"Maurice!"

He jumped out of bed and ran out of his bedroom and ran to her.

She was complaining of dizziness and severe chest pain.

Maurice asked her gently what her symptoms were.

His mother once again mentioned the dizziness, but most worrisome, the severe chest pain.

He asked her if she wanted to go to the hospital and she adamantly and forcibly said "No!".

Maurice was worried and returned to his bedroom pacing back and forth.

Once again, he returned to her bedroom and the symptoms were the same.

Sharron, his mother, was a very authoritarian figure his life.

Maurice, determined, told her he would call the emergency medical services also known as 9-1-1.

She panicked and pleaded to him not to do so.

Out of worry, he went against her wishes and called.

The phone operator at 9-1-1 asked what the emergency was.

He nervously told her that his mother had chest pains and was afraid she may be having a heart attack.

Maurice made the right decision as he did not want to be responsible or feel guilty for an ill demise.

He quickly dressed, pulled on a pair of pants, a top that was previously pressed the night before and combed his hair as to not look like a lunatic.

He wore a light jacket.

He sprayed on his favorite eau de toilette.

All of this was automatic, he was prepared to accompany his mother onto an ambulance vehicle.

He looked for all of her medicine bottles and carefully put them into a plastic bag to explain her medical history at the hospital.

Within minutes, he heard the sirens and through the windows saw the red and yellow lights from vehicles.

Maurice's telephone rang, announcing that the emergency personnel were by the door and to let them in.

He did.

He was confused, as initially the fire department personnel, about six men, rushed into the apartment.

They carefully and diligently walked throughout the apartment.

Out of nervousness, Maurice, lit a cigarette and was commanded by the fire department to shut it out.

He abided, although angry, extinguished the cigarette by the kitchen sink.

So much was going on at a fast pace.

Next, the EMT's, followed the perceived fire fighters with emergency equipment at hand.

They rushed to Sharon's bedside and initiated tests and exams to see her health condition.

There were two EMT's.

Both calm and collected.

One sat down to ask Maurice about Sharon's medical history and the other took out medical equipment to start testing on Sharon.

The latter had a backpack with portable EKG machines, blood pressure equipment and also diabetic paraphernalia to test the patients' blood sugar levels.

They were both professional, yet, had a good bed side manner.

Sharon was agitated as she thought she would be going to the hospital.

She told the technician that she was fine and that he was ugly.

It was amusing, but they were accustomed to this type of behavior from patients in an agitated state.

The "ugly" one took Sharon's blood pressure and it was a bit high, normal for a person that was feeling very nervous.

He proceeded to conduct the EKG test, modern technology, and it did not note any signs of heart attack.

It was normal.

He then lightly punctured her finger to get a blood sample as she had a history of diabetes.

He did this twice and she cursed at him.

He laughed and tried to make her feel comfortable.

The other EMT laughed as he understood the Spanish foul expletives that came out of her mouth.

Maurice stayed back, allowing the emergency personnel do their job.

He was certainly nervous.

The EMT's strongly recommended that she should go to the hospital for further testing.

She said "No!".

I want to stay home.

She hated hospitals and doctors, she proclaimed to them.

They once again explained the importance of further testing, but she forcibly declined.

They abided by her wishes since the at home testing was "normal".

The EMT's stated that if Sharon was taken to the hospital and she stated she was feeling fine, they would send her home without question.

Since the patient was fully aware, they couldn't question her health status and would have to let her go back home.

She was told to sign on a laptop that she declined further assistance and her son Maurice signed as witness.

Protocol, that was all.

They pleasantly said their goodbyes and told Maurice that if anything else happened to not hesitate to call again.

Maurice, remembered in hindsight, that one of the EMT's was creeped out by Sharon's treasured dolls which she called her children.

He disliked lifelike dolls.

Maurice assumed that this kind EMT was traumatized by dolls at one time or another in his life.

That must be another story.

Once the EMT's left, Maurice sat by his mother's side and tried to calm her down.
He decided to give her a sedative, so that she could relax and sleep soundly.

She did relax and asked him to accompany her to the bathroom so that she could urinated.

He walked her and waited outside of the bathroom door.

She sorts of forgot about the incident and he explained the whole situation.

Maurice worried before going to bed, that this would only be one of similar situations.

He was content that he took the upper hand and called 9-1-1.

Maurice will no longer hesitate in the future.

He loves his mother, and nothing will ever hold him back from intervening for her wellbeing.

Caring for one's parent or parents is not easy, but it is a responsibility.

A MOTHER'S LOSS

The senior woman does a great job of donning a mask,

hiding an insufferable pain that will not leave her ever.

She's been doing this decade after decade.

To her, it only seems like yesterday.

In the course of nature as we believe it,

the abominable occurrence in her life should have never taken place.

Evil prevailed.

Her young son, an innocent 22-year young man, full of life and promise,

was murdered.

He was shot by a gun twice.

Once in the arm and finally on his head.

The latter being the deadly blow.

He did fight for his life with courage and bravery brought on by
adrenaline.

The criminals were clients he trusted and served often.

That moment in time, forever, frozen in time, was not expected.

He was a victim of crime.

Shot in the arm and head by ruthless, low life robbers.

The criminals thought that the young man had large amounts of money
and jewelry in his home.

Why?

The young man was a hard worker climbing the ladder of success in the
corporate world.

On a part time basis, he also legally sold and bought gold from his home and had a loyal clientele base.

He had a beautiful girlfriend that he intended to marry.

Just in a few minutes, all was shattered.

He lost his life.

The mother, brother, distanced father and all relatives lost a beautiful loved one.

It was traumatizing for his girlfriend as well as she witnessed the horrendous crime.

She was the star witness at the trial months later.

She had to bravely yet sadly, recount all that she witnessed on that summer day.

Although life went on for all, it did not for the family members.

The criminals were caught shortly thereafter the crime as his girlfriend was able to identify them.

They served time in jail, but, not enough.

One of the assailing criminals, the one that pulled the trigger of the gun, died in jail of a terminal illness.

The jail time, the death of the assailant that pulled the trigger, was not enough.

Justice would never be served.

An innocent life full of promise was lost forever.

He will always be remembered.

Fortunately, the grieving mother had her younger son, that adored her as much as the son she lost but can never replace him.

The grieving mother could not and would never forget that her first born was no longer alive.

The young son was always expressing his love to her.

Hugging and kissing her and asking for her blessings.

As the years passed, the pain numbed, but was always present.

Decades later, she still asks, what could she have done to protect her son.

Mothers are like that, right?

Protecting her children even as they become adults.

Providing wisdom and answering their questions and doubts.

Providing comfort to their child.

This horrific incident, frozen in time, will forever be recorded in her mind, heart and soul until she leaves this earthly plane.

At times, due to the years she carries, she calls for him forgetting that he is gone.

By the law of nature, more frequently than not, the children outlive their parents.

May one day both mother and son be reunited with love in the celestial heavens.

AUTUMN LEAF

It was a blustery rainy cool autumn day.

The skies were a menacing dark gray, as if a heavy downpour was about to hit the ground.

A light rain as they walked

Nonetheless, Zoe and Colton, were enjoying the cool day, sheltering themselves with umbrellas.

They were not in a rush as they walked the city blocks.

Their get together to have lunch at a local restaurant.

Carrying on lighthearted conversations and laughing as they walked.

There were heavy wet tree leaves laying on the street before them.

It was a windy day as well.

Suddenly, Colton saw something peculiar coming from behind their backs on the street block.

A single lightweight leaf skipping the ground.

It made leaps and bounds as if it were dancing in the rain.

It moved from left to right, right to left, up and down.

Colton was mesmerized by this leaf.

The leaf did not have a care in the world.

It was enjoying itself.

If leaves could sing, this one certainly would.

It was a light maple color with hues of orange and brown.

Colton wondered where this magical leaf came from.

Zoe had no idea or insight as to what Colton was seeing or perceiving.

Colton was conversing yet, with his vivid imagination was enjoying the sight of this leaf.

It was such a joy.

Where was this leaf going?

It swirled with happiness enjoying the rain and wind, with no specific destination in mind.

Colton found this to be marvelous.

Something, a sight, which he never witnessed.

A leaf dancing in the rain.

Any other person would not perceive what Colton did.

Yet, Colton did.

This filled Colton with a childlike happiness.

As he continued to converse with his best friend,

his eyes followed the leaf just ahead of him.

Oh, what conversations Colton wanted to have with this lovely leaf.

Out of all leaves laying sullen and dead on the ground, this was a leaf full of an unnatural magical life.

Not allowing the rain to ruin his unknown destination.

It hopped, sprang and rose in the cool air.

A magical dance indeed.

Then a power gust came along and swished this leaf further down the street,

until it could not be seen by Colton's eyes any longer.

A brief moment in time, that would be imprinted in Colton's life forever.

Colton continued his talk with Zoe, holding on tight to their umbrellas.

Zoe need not know the pleasure Colton experienced for a few moments as they walked.

It was his secret which he could revisit in his mind when feeling the blues.

Oh my, such a wonderful leaf.

He wished he could grab on to the leaf and safely put it in one of the pockets of his bright yellow rain jacket to bring home.

Colton would certainly keep it in a safe place, perhaps a solid bright yellow dish to admire from time to time.

It sounds a bit bizarre, but this leaf made his day.

It brought him immense joy.

A single leaf full of life, music and dance.

Perhaps, he'll see a similar leaf again before winter banishes them.

Autumn leaf.

An autumn leaf full of magical properties deeply affecting a human mind.

Until next time, autumn leaf.

BELOVED MOTHER

There are no words sufficient enough that can describe how much I love you.

As a child you taught me the meaning of love, values, morals and respect.

When in school, you were always there to support my efforts and applaud my achievements.

You played a very important part of my life in my upbringing.

Education.

Work.

Spirituality.

Although you divorced my father at an age where I was very young, you compensated for the lack of my father's presence.

You were both Mother and Father.

You took on dual roles.

I admit I was not an angel, just like many children growing up.

You were stern and expected the best for me.

I apologize if I ever hurt you in anyway.

I was smart in class yet was loud and funny.

Distracting other students who laughed along with me.

My teachers, although at times annoyed with my behavior, understood me.

I was one of the class clowns, but a smart clown.

You ensured that my homework was done after school and submitted to my teachers on a timely basis.

You patiently helped me with assignments if I had questions.

I could see your proud smile when I completed my studies.

I didn't go to college right after High School.

Do you know why?

I wanted to work to help you with the family bills.

I didn't feel it was fair for you to have that burden on your shoulders of paying for my education.

Therefore, I worked and went to college part time.

It took me longer than my peers to graduate from college, but I made it.

I thank you!

Thank you for the unending loving you gave me and my beloved brother.

You were so protective.

When there were other boys bullying me, you were the first to confront them and their parents to make it stop.

I thank you.

You taught me how to protect myself and not allow others to bully me.

You told me to "Hit them with anything and knock them out! They will learn and not bully you anymore. They will not fear you, but they will respect you".

Thank you, Mom.

My chosen professional career was in international corporate banking.

I thrived and climbed up the ladder.

On the side, I wrote poems and prose.

Writing was my love and continues to be.

Initially, I kept the writing to myself.

Now, I share it with the world.

Thank you, Mom, for always being there and guiding me in life.

You also encouraged me to continue writing and to share it with those that would appreciate it.

During my childhood and as an adult, spirituality played a very important role in my life as well.

I was fascinated by all religions and spiritual paths.

I followed several, learned and kept the positive aspects of my spiritual exploring.

Thank you, Mom for being supportive in my spiritual and religious quests, allowing me to be me.

Mom, thank you for being you.

I love you just as you are and that will never change.

You are my Beloved Mom.

QUERIDA MADRE

No hay palabras suficientes que puedan describir cuánto te amo.

De niño me enseñaste el significado del amor, los valores, la moral y el respeto.

Cuando estabas en la escuela, siempre estabas allí para apoyar mis esfuerzos y aplaudir mis logros.

Tuviste una parte muy importante de mi vida en mi educación.

Educación.

Trabajo.

Espiritualidad.

Aunque te divorciaste de mi padre a una edad en la que yo era muy joven, compensaste la falta de la presencia de mi padre.

Eras madre y padre.

Asumiste papeles duales.

Admito que no era un ángel, como muchos niños que crecen.

Eras estricta y esperabas lo mejor para mí.

Pido disculpas si alguna vez te lastimé en esta vida.

Yo era inteligente en clase, pero era ruidoso y divertido.

Distrayendo a otros estudiantes que se rieron junto a mí.

Mis maestros, aunque a veces molestos con mi comportamiento, me entendieron.

Yo era uno de los payasos de la clase, pero un payaso inteligente.

Aseguraste de que mi tarea se hiciera después de la escuela y se presentara a mis maestros de manera oportuna.

Pacientemente me ayudaste con mis tareas si yo tenía preguntas.

Pude ver tu sonrisa orgullosa cuando terminé mis estudios.

No fui a la universidad justo después de la secundaria.

¿Sabes por qué?

Quería trabajar para ayudarte con las facturas familiares.

No sentí que fuera justo para ti tener esa carga sobre tus hombros de pagar mi educación.

Por lo tanto, trabajé y fui a la universidad a tiempo parcial.

Me tomó más tiempo que mis compañeros graduarme de la universidad, pero lo logré.

¡Te lo agradezco!

Gracias por el amor infinita que me diste a mí y a mi querido hermano.

Fuiste muy protectora.

Cuando había otros niños que me acosaban, tú eras el primero en confrontarlos a ellos y a sus padres para detenerlo.

Te lo agradezco.

Me enseñaste cómo protegerme y no permitir que otros me intimiden.

Me dijiste que "¡Golpea con cualquier cosa y noquea! Aprenderán y no te intimidarán más. No te temerán, pero te respetarán".

Gracias, mami.

Mi carrera profesional elegida fue en la banca corporativa internacional.

Prosperé y subí la escalera de éxito.

Por un lado, escribí poemas y prosa.

Escribir fue mi amor y seguí haciéndolo.

Inicialmente, me guardé la escritura.

Ahora lo comparto con el mundo.

Gracias, mamá por estar siempre allí y guiarme en la vida.

También me alentaste a seguir escribiendo y a compartirlo con aquellos que lo apreciarían.

Durante mi infancia y como adulto, la espiritualidad también jugó un papel muy importante en mi vida.

Estaba fascinado por todas las religiones y caminos espirituales.

Seguí a varios, aprendí y mantuve los aspectos positivos de mi exploración espiritual.

Gracias, mamá por apoyarme en mis búsquedas espirituales y religiosas, permitiéndome ser yo.

Mamá, gracias por ser tú.

Te amo tal como eres y eso nunca cambiará.

Eres mi amada mamá.

BLACK OUT

He was sitting on the examination bed, slouched over.

Waiting for the test results.

Humpty Dumpty sat on a wall.

Humpty Dumpty had a great fall.

The urgent care room felt so cold.

Not the staff, just the room temperature which made the waiting much more uncomfortable.

Poor Charlie.

He had no idea he'd end up in this room due to his "great fall".

A couple of days earlier, Charlie was sitting on his chair by his computer desk.

In the wee hours of the morning, contemplating as he was unable to sleep.

Bang, boom!

He slipped off the chair, crashing hard onto the cold wooden floor.

He can't recall what prompted the fall.

Sleepiness?

Dizziness?

When Charlie got up from the fall, he had blood all over his face.

He ran into the bathroom to wash and wipe his face.

There was a deep gash above his right eyebrow.

Although the first logical thought to go to the emergency room at a nearby hospital, it was not a viable option.

He cared for his sick sibling and could not leave her alone.

Charlie did not sleep at all the rest of the night.

He was afraid that due to the fall and banging his head he may go into a concussion.

Charlie applied pressure to the wound to stop the bleeding.

Applied an antibiotic ointment and dressed it with a band aid.

During the same day, during daylight hours, he contacted his primary doctor to recount this unexplainable incident.

His doctor was very concerned and told him to go to the hospital emergency room for assessment.

Hardheaded Charlie did not want to go as he knew that he would be waiting long hours as most folk experience in emergency rooms.

Poor Charlie.

He waited two days to finally go to an urgency care facility.

Less waiting time.

As he waited to be seen, he started to recall his fall.

Humpty Dumpty sat on the wall.

Humpty Dumpty had a great fall.

Although Charlie had that great fall, he knew he would recover.

The physicians at the urgency care center were carefully asking his medical history and noted the medications he was prescribed by his primary doctor.

The physicians concluded that Charlie, blacked out and should go to hospital for further testing and evaluation.

Charlie refused as he wanted to go back home and take care of his sibling.

His sibling was very important to him.

He forgoes his care in order to take care of her.

Charlie would certainly learn from this experience.

The lesson for him was not to wake up in the middle of the night and sit on his chair.

He did not want to blackout again and have a serious injury.

Poor Charlie, called his primary doctor once again to make an appointment to treat this injury.

The doctor scolded him lightly and told him that if he wakes up in the middle of the night, to sit on his bed for a few minutes to gather his baring's.

He heeded the doctor's advice and never sat on that computer chair in the middle wee hours of the night.

Charlie did not want to experience the same as before.

Humpty Dumpty had a great fall.

Unlike the nursery rhyme, Humpty Dumpty was put together whole once again.

Lessons to be learned from a hardheaded man named Charlie.

Charlie is fine now.

He'll never play with fate again.

Lessons to be learned in life.

BRIELLA

It was not unusual for a witch of her power to desire sleep as most humans do.

Briella was very special indeed.

She has lived five centuries.

Father Time was kind to her.

She has a porcelain smooth silky skin without any signs of aging.

Long black lustrous, shiny, straight hair who's length if below her buttocks.

One would think Briella was at a day spa frequently.

No, that was not the case.

All her physical gifts were bestowed upon her by the Greek God Apollo.

She had beautiful dark eyes, a very dark brown, which appeared to the public as black.

Briella was a very a powerful, beautiful, intelligent and talented witch.

She has the gift of prophecy, clairvoyance.

When she looks upon a person, she is able to see their entire past, present and future.

Briella is cautious of what she tells people when in a prophetic state.

Not everyone will comprehend her gift, therefore, some will be afraid of her.

She is benevolent and has seen both good and evil during her long lifetime.

Briella, as not to be recognized by other people with clairvoyant gifts, created a protective shield of sorts.

This shield did not allow those of her own kind see her as a witch but a simple human.

She is masterful in her art of magic.

Apollo taught her well.

Back to her sleeping pattern.

She only slept a few hours a night.

Enough to refresh her body and mind.

Afterall, she was the undead amongst the living.

Her favorite color of clothing is black.

With all the riches she accumulated during her lifetime, she could afford the finest clothing.

Dior, Chanelle, Louis Vuitton, Prada and Armani just to name a few.

Due to her charm, these designers both living and dead, many were delighted to gift clothing.

Finely tailored clothes to fit her slim body.

She truly appreciated their kind gestures.

Briella is very charming and has a delicate look about herself.

During the centuries lived, she was a witness to an evolving world.

Peace and war.

Sleeping by candlelight in the early late sixteenth century to bright electrical lighting in the twentieth century.

She made many enduring friendships during her lifetime, including members of royalty from various continents.

The royal courts welcomed her with open majestic doors.

The British, French, Spanish and African courts of loyalty adored her.

The Kings, Queens, Princesses and Princes loved her.

They saw her through a lens, which saw her as royalty as well.

Royal members enjoyed sitting down with her sipping tea to hear her charming tales.

They were magically charmed by Briella.

Briella travelled quite a lot.

Travelling via steamships to modern day airplanes.

Briella ate the finest foods and most expensive wines.

She lived and continues to live a luxurious life.

The God Apollo gifted her with immortality.

At times she contemplated whether it was a gift or a curse.

She lived to bury her longtime beloved friends.

That was the sad part of the gift.

Her outliving her friends.

Peculiarly, they never questioned why she did not age physically.

They knew intuitively, that she had a gift and was probably not of the human species.

Nonetheless, her friends loved her without prejudice or fear.

Briella had the most interesting conversations with her friends.

Love.

Her many adventures in life.

Her friends loved her stories.

Some wondered if what she narrated was true or false.

They didn't care.

Briella was a brilliant young woman that amused and charmed them.

Due to the gift of immortality, there were moments of unhappiness and loneliness.

She saw her friends both be born and die.

Immortality was more of a curse than a gift.

She cursed Apollo for bestowing this "gift" upon her.

Apollo smiled from the celestial heavens.

Briella wanted to be normal like every human being.

She didn't need the gift of prophecy; she could live happily without it.

Yet, she found this gift amusing and so did her friends.

All of her friends admired the three-karat emerald ring on her left ring finger.

It sparkled during the night and day.

The ring was put on her finger by Apollo.

At times she attempted to remove the ring, but it was magically attached.

Unremovable.

A reminder of immortality.

A gesture of marriage to the God.

Briella will continue her adventures and continue to befriend people of her stature.

The never-ending life.

Briella.

BUTTERFLY

She had a revelatory dream, where she dreamt with a beautiful butterfly.

A butterfly with multiple colors from a rainbow spectrum.

A butterfly that flapped its wings and stayed in place.

The most peculiar part of the dream was that the butterfly was sitting upon a beautiful wooden casket.

A coffin.

Yes, a coffin that was crafted of cherrywood and the lighting in the room, shined brilliant pink hues.

She did not feel uncomfortable at all.

No fright, no fear.

There was no one else in the viewing room of the funeral parlor.

She felt a sense of peace, knowing that there were changes to come.

The closed casket represented the end of emotional and mental pain that her plagued her for many years.

She welcomed it.

The colorful butterfly represented positive changes to come soon.

A positive transformation in all aspects of her life.

She embraced all of this, although a dream.

She woke up from this dream, feeling refreshed and at peace.

A deep cleansing breath and beautiful smile.

She realized that the pain she went through in life, which was repetitive in love relationships, were a learning experience.

The disenchantment she had, was a learning experience, not to be repeated.

She has a heart of gold, a strong woman and deserves the best.

We learn in life and experience pain and love.

We cannot look back at the painful experiences, as it is what it is.

We just learn.

No to conformation, no one should conform just to have a companion by your side.

Conformity is toxic.

No repetition, looking forward to finding that special person that will appreciate us.

In this scenario, a man that will appreciate her virtues and the love she has to give.

She thanks the Divine, for such a beautiful dream.

She will survive, live, love and move forward in life.

Such is love.

Young lady, fly, fly, fly just like the butterfly.

CARLEEN AND STEVEN

Carleen was contemplating her life,

past and present.

She's at an elderly age and recalling all that her memory has stored.

Carleen fondly remembers her childhood.

She was a daddy's girl.

Her father always showered her with love.

Tickled her little belly as a child and she would burst out with laughter.

Her mother was just as loving.

Carleen's mother passed away at an early age of a terminal disease, throat cancer.

At the age of twenty-eight.

Carleen was only nine years old, but still has the memory of her mother's smile and naturally curly brunette hair.

Her mother was a beauty.

It was a travesty that she died at such a young age.

Carleen's father grieved yet had to be strong to take care of his only child.

Carleen.

She was the most important part of his life since his wife's unexpected death.

He made do.

His two sisters helped in the caregiving of his beautiful daughter.

Carleen performed very well in school and went to study foreign languages at the university.

She made her father proud.

When she finished her studies, she served as a prominent translator at the United Nations.

That is where she met her first and only love.

His name is Steven.

A man of integrity and humility that demonstrated love to Carleen in so many ways.

Within one year they married.

Carleen and Steven decided to move to Forest Hills, Queens County in NYC.

The neighborhood was beautiful and access to all amenities.

Restaurants, small quaint art galleries and above all, friendly neighbors.

They were very amicable; it was very easy to make long lasting friendships.

He was very much like her father.

Handsome, intelligent and very much giving.

Unfortunately, they were not able to bare children.

They sadly accepted this situation.

Nonetheless, they adored each other.

The love they would impart to the children they wanted; they did unto themselves.

It was a lovely relationship they had.

When it came to vacations, they travelled all over the world.

They held hands and showed loving affection in public, without a care in the world.

It just came naturally to them.

Carleen's father, unfortunately, died at the early age of sixty in his sleep.

Doctor's indicated that he had an undetected heart condition.

Carleen, once again, was heartbroken.

She lost the father that raised her on his own and showered her with love.

Steven was very fond of her father as well.

Steven was there for Carleen at every moment possible through the grieving period.

It was not an easy period in her life.

First her mother, then her father.

In the back of her mind, she questioned, who next would depart her side.

Life is so bizarre.

One day we are happy and the next, catastrophe strikes.

Little did she know, that death was right around the corner, once again.

Steven was assigned a business trip to Germany.

A very important meeting he had to attend related to his line of work.

He was excited as he never been to this part of Europe was looking forward to the few days there.

Of course, he would miss Carleen, but the trip was short and would see her soon enough on his return.

Steven arrived two hours early at Kennedy Airport to check in and board the airplane.

All went smoothly.

When it was time for takeoff from the airport hangar, the airplane had drastic mechanical problems.

The airplane started to ascend, and the baggage compartment contained luggage which illegally had unstable lithium batteries in an electronic device.

The device caught on fire which spread rapidly throughout the baggage compartment.

It was out of control.

The pilots saw the alarms and alarmingly contacted the control tower at the airport to return and descend.

It was too late.

The smoke from the fire reached the passenger compartment.

There was smoke all over the place.

The plane turned around to attempt a safe landing, but it was too late.

The tail end of the plain caught on fire and exploded in midair.

Casualties.

No survivors.

Steven perished along with all passengers, pilots and airline personnel.

Large and small pieces of debris covered the runway.

It was a horrible sight to see.

The proper governmental authorities investigated on sight.

The TSA, FBI, Fire Firefighter and Police arrived expeditiously.

It was determined that there was no foul play.

In a short period of time, family members of the passengers were contacted and informed of the demised.

Very sad.

The passengers were identified by their DNA.

Steven.

When Carleen was informed, she couldn't believe what had occurred.

She broke down in tears of sorrow, of loss.

Her beloved was gone.

Carleen's friends offered support and comfort.

It took a long time for Carleen to grasp her loss and try to move on.

Not an easy thing to do.

One day, she woke up and decided that she would never love again.

She would remain single for the rest of her life.

In her mind, there was no reason to be with anyone else.

She felt cursed.

All the important people in her life were taken away and she would not take that chance again.

She returned to work after the bereavement period and focused on just that.

Going to work and returning to her empty home.

The latter happened for years until she retired.

She would sit on her bed and contemplate her life.

There were times where she thought about ending her life.

She came to her senses and logically decided that she would wait for her time to leave world.

She looked forward to seeing once again her love, Steven, in heaven.

In the meantime, she waited as patiently as she could.

The day arrived; she was heartbroken.

She died of heart break as she sat on her bed.

No physical pain, her heart gave out, just like her father.

No more pain.

No more loneliness.

When her soul left her body, Steven was present to welcome her, to continue their love relationship in the heavens.

She was at peace.

No more pain.

Just, a celestial reunion with her love and eternal peace.

That is true love.

CHANTELLE

Chantelle is a beautiful young lady, both outwardly and inwardly.

Long dark wavy hair, green eyes that shined as if they were smiling and a beautiful body.

Her parents were not the best.

They were abusers.

Both physically and emotionally.

She had other siblings, but they were treated differently.

With love and admiration.

Chantelle, during childhood age did not know why her parents treated her so badly.

She was the most beautiful and intelligent of all her siblings.

Her siblings loved her, but they could not protect her from her parents.

There was something special about her that her parents did not like nor voiced out loud.

Nonetheless, she excelled in school to try to make her parents proud.

The parents scoffed and paid no attention to her achievements.

This was very painful for her but did not allow it to impede her life's goals.

She actually wanted to be an entertainer; she had a beautiful sing voice.

Chantelle, an appropriate name for a singer.

That went unnoticed as well.

She had the look of a runway model.

Perhaps that was a reason her parents despised her.

They saw what they couldn't see in themselves.

Eventually, she graduated from high school with great grades.

Unfortunately, her parents did not support her desire to pursue a higher education.

She was naïve as a teenager and did not pursue the educational goals she actually wanted as she did not have the financial resources to attend.

Chantelle started to work as a waitress at a high-end restaurant.

The owners saw promise in her and knew her beauty would bring in more clients at the bar.

Low and behold, many clients started making this restaurant very popular due to her presence.

She saved as much money as possible with the salary and tips she received as a bartender.

With that money, she finally moved out of her parents' home and found a studio apartment.

The rent was a struggle for her.

But at last, she was free from the abuse from her parents.

She kept in contact with her beloved siblings.

One day, a client that was frequently at the restaurant told her that she can make much more money in another way.

He invited her to lunch to discuss.

A business proposal.

She had no idea he was a pimp, a man that had beautiful girls sell their bodies in exchange for sex.

Chantelle, with low self-esteem due to her upbringing, decided to try it.

She did.

She walked the streets of New York City as a prostitute.

Her attire was sexy yet tasteful.

She was high end.

Her makeup was extraordinarily beautifully applied.

She started to attract clients and many of them were repeat clients.

Chantelle was a goddess.

Initially she was anxious and nervous about her new gig, but eventually got accustomed.

Her pimp, was always protective and vigilant of her, ensuring she would not get hurt by "Johns".

He falsely demonstrated a father figure that she always wanted.

His commission was thirty percent of what she made each day.

She made so much money, that she was able to get a one-bedroom apartment in a high-rise building in a desirable neighborhood in the city.

Chantelle, with all this money, decorated her apartment with beautiful furniture.

Her new home.

A steady line of clients, and she gave them the sexual satisfaction they needed.

One night, she hit the city streets to do her job and was picked up in a luxury car by a "John".

He appeared to be friendly but Chantelle, naïve as she was could not detect his sinister intention.

This John hated women, he had his own psychological issues and trauma.

He wanted to hurt beautiful ladies.

When she entered the car with a beautiful smile, he smiled in return.

He saw a goddess and his intent was to hurt her.

They drove off to a street that was desolate and dark.

When she attempted to touch him, he punched her in the face repeatedly.

He continued to abuse her, like her father, but much worse.

She screamed and fought back as best as she could, but no one could hear her.

There was blood underneath her nails from scratching his face.

Her pimp had no idea where she was, therefore, could not save her.

The John's last punch was on her forehead and she passed out.

He had no idea the damage he did to her.

It was a fatal blow.

When he shook her to wake up, she did not.

He realized that he killed her.

He realized, that no one could know what he did.

He drove away from the initial location and found another dark street.

Pulled her out of the car and laid her body on the sidewalk and drove off.

He was a mess, but worse off, he had the blood of a lady of the night in his hands.

The next morning, her body was found by young woman walking by the same sidewalk.

She screamed.

She saw Chantelle's terribly bruised face.

She saw that she was not breathing.

Right away, the young woman went into her purse and pulled out her cell phone to call for help.

The police and ambulance arrived within minutes.

Chantelle was pronounced dead.

Chantelle, a young lady full of promise, was gone forever.

Her family was informed of the awful incident by the police.

Even then, her parents showed no emotional remorse.

Eventually, they will have to deal and confront the death of their goddess daughter.

Rest in peace, Chantelle.

CHARACTERS ENCOUNTERED ON A SUMMER DAY

He did not imagine, what a fascinating late summer afternoon it would be,

after his scheduled meeting in the historic cobbled streets of lower Manhattan.

The meeting went rather well.

Pleasantries exchanged and down to good old business.

It ended on a very good note and enough time to savor the sunshine and breeze during a heatwave that

approached the city.

Although it was a heatwave, the weather wasn't uncomfortable at all.

A nice breeze in the shade was flowing through the streets of the city.

He had the appropriate light cotton shirt on to keep cool.

As he left the towering edifice where the meeting was held,

he encountered many different characters.

You see, he is very observant with an imaginative mind.

As he walked along John Street,

there was a handsome black man, he appeared healthy and strong.

Yet, the man was pandering for money to get a bite to eat.

He asked the man leaving the meeting if he would spare fifty cents.

The man, being empathetic, walked a few steps back and returned to the man asking for money and gave him a dollar.

The smile on the other man was priceless and full of gratitude.

He continued walking several city blocks to the NYC subway,

the Cortlandt train station to be precise.

As he walked down the stair steps to the train he wanted to board, he saw gift shops for tourists, candy and newspaper stands.

It was a long time since he had been in this part of the city.

He swiped the MetroCard to pay his fare at the most appropriate time.

The train was just pulling into the train station and he boarded the train.

Afternoon crowds of people leaving work and others eagerly waiting to get onboard to reach their destinations.

Once on board, there was a window seat next to an elderly lady.

It was going to be a long train ride for him, and he politely excused himself, asked the lady's pardon to sit next to her.

She kindly obliged.

What a relief to sit he thought and was grateful.

At the next station, a slew of passengers boarded.

Whew, he was thankful he had a seat.

He noticed, sitting across from him, a mother and child.

The mother was preoccupied with her thoughts and cellphone.

The young child was looking through her bejeweled backpack for chewing gum.

Once she found the gum, she sighed and proceeded to indulge.

Not only that, she also had a tech device, a notepad and was typing away, she could've been playing a game or just writing.

There was no visible communication between the mother and child during the train ride.

They were both preoccupied with their devices.

They only communicated, more like a nudge on the shoulder when they had to get off at their train stop destination.

Just about everyone had a cellphone, typing away, listening to music, oblivious to their surroundings.

One interesting character, a man of tall stature entered the train at the Court Street station.

He was dressed casually and well groomed.

His eyes were bright and alert.

What stood out was that he was carrying a starred badge on his waist and had a gun secured in its holster.

Perhaps, a correction officer or court officer.

The man observing all of this found it strange that the officer was displaying the gun publicly on a train.

He made no effort to hide it until children boarded the train at the next station.

Then he discreetly covered the holster with a newspaper.

Another character.

As the train ride progressed, more and more people boarded.

One man with short pants, bearded that appeared to be in his late thirties was dancing as he stood by one of the subway doors.

But he didn't have earphones.

Apparently, he was dancing to the music playing in his mind.

This passenger is enjoying life, isn't he?

So many interesting characters we encounter in our daily lives.

Whether walking in the street or riding in the subway or buses.

The observer finally got off at his home destination station.

He saw the familiar token booth clerk he always sees.

She waved and smiled at him and he did the same.

He walked up the stairs out to the street.

Eager to get back to his air-conditioned apartment.

Of course, he saw other interesting characters on his way home in his neighborhood.

That's another story for some other time.

You just have to love all types of characters you encounter on a daily basis.

CHARLIE

Who is this captivating, charming young man named Charlie?

He has the all-American "boy" next door look.

He is an only child.

Adopted as a baby by loving parents.

Red wavy hair, crystalline blue eyes, of very fair complexion with light freckles.

Impeccably dressed.

Always well-groomed from head to toe.

One of his favorite colors must be white, as he always wears finely tailored white dress shirts, with sharp crisp creases on the sleeves.

A smile that is most inviting to those that he meets.

Very friendly and sociable.

He greets all his colleagues with a cheerful "Good morning!" a firm handshake and smile.

A great conversationalist.

He always has a fascinating tale to tell.

He enters a board room and all eyes are on him.

Appealing to all, women and men.

Many have secret crushes.

He appears to be a great catch.

His profession is within the U.S. corporate world.

He climbed the latter of success quickly, a result of long hours and hard work at the renowned American company with offices worldwide.

Yet, there is something about him that is hard to pinpoint.

He appears to be a as mentioned, the "boy" next door.

But there is something that he hides.

A secret.

Another life, unbeknownst to his friends, colleagues and family.

Who is the real Charlie?

What does he hide?

What about him is he not revealing to those that are apparently close to him?

A money launderer?

A government agent spy?

He works in the corporate financial industry.

What else is he doing during the long hours at work when unsupervised?

He has access to confidential computer codes that are only assigned to people of his highly visible position.

Perhaps he was embedded by the U.S. government into this financial company to see if there is corruption.

He was hired by this company seamlessly and highly recommended.

A foreign agent perhaps hired by cynical foreign governments.

He wears a mask, figuratively.

He's very intelligent and knows his way around this company.

A double agent?

Time will tell when his identity is discovered.

All is revealed in due time.

A matter of time.

Who is Charlie?

We will know who Charlie truly is, wishing sooner than later.

Hopefully before anything nefarious and dark occurs.

Who is Charlie?

COVERED BY ROSES

Ah, there is nothing like the scent of roses.

The texture of rose petals is very special too.

A silky comforting feel on your skin.

Red, pink, yellow, lavender colored roses are extraordinary.

There are some hybrids as well, but not with that heavenly scent of the original roses.

The eau de toilette and perfumes with the overtones of roses are intoxicating in a heavenly way.

The smell takes you to a celestial dimension.

Yes, the magic of roses.

It would be wonderful to lay on a bed covered totally with pink and red roses.

What do the roses represent to you?

Love?

Comfort?

Sensuality?

Perhaps all the above and more.

No matter the cost, it would be ecstatic to covered by a multitude of rose petals while you sleep.

It will certainly bring you peace.

A sense of love and being loved.

This desire is wished by that single man or woman awaiting love from a special person.

Until that lover manifests, the roses will do.

A blanket of roses caressing their body.

Fantasizing that special love will arrive sooner or later.

In the meantime, the special flower representing love will do.

Roses, roses, roses.

Bathed in roses, covered by roses in bed.

Wearing a special scent of roses reminding them that true love will be around the corner.

The rose fragrance in the perfumes will remind them of love and peace.

Hoping that the special person will manifest in their life soon.

In the interim, the fragrant roses will do until the Prince or Princess comes along.

The love of your life.

It would be wonderful if a bed blanket made of real scent roses are available to cuddle as you sleep.

Yes, that would be magical indeed.

Don't give up.

Allow hope to stay alive as that special person will arrive.

In the meantime, the roses will cover you with love and not ask nothing in return.

The roses job will take care of you in your waiting period.

Magnificent roses, that is what they are.

Tonight, I will anoint myself with a rose fragrance and sleep peacefully bringing about sweet dreams.

Sweet dreams to my love to be, I patiently wait for you.

DEEP SLEEP

Joseph had a long day at work.

Worked over 12 hours attending to clients via text, telephone and video conference calls.

He was a valuable and respected colleague at work.

Joseph was in the busy finance industry.

He barely had time to eat lunch, usually took half an hour to chow down food and have a cup of coffee.

Although he was accustomed to his line of work, it was wearing him down.

Afterall, he's been in this line of work for almost 20 years.

Yet, he enjoyed his line of work and had no intentions to change careers.

He usually started his day at seven am eastern standard time due to European clients.

His clients adored him as he was very diligent and got the work done in a timely fashion.

This one day, he left at seven pm as usual.

The public transportation was prompt and he arrived home within half an hour.

Time to whine down before eating dinner.

He changed into more comfortable attire and took a deep breath before ordering takeout food.

Today, it was a generous portion of healthy food.

Freshly grilled chicken and a mixed salad with plenty of greens and a balsamic vinaigrette to accompany it.

He was satisfied with his meal.

Although at home, he always watched the pertinent financial news to apply for the following day.

After watching the news, he took a warm relaxing shower.

As the pulsating water hit his body, he allowed himself to relax.

It was much needed.

He changed to terry white shorts and a t-shirt.

Joseph decided to call it an early night and went to bed.

Effortlessly, he went into a deep sleep.

Deep sleep.

A joyful deep sleep.

Although he rarely remembered his dreams,

this was a type of sleep pattern where he would.

The dream was about his childhood.

He was fortunate to have two wonderful parents.

His mother Grace and father James.

He had a wonderful childhood, full of memories.

The dream was very vivid.

In the public playground, his father James, sitting him on the swings.

Pushing the swing back and forth, delighted that his son, Joseph was gleeful and enjoying this time with him.

Deep sleep.

The dream fluidly continued.

His mother Grace had the dining table set up with an array of delightful and tasty food.

Deep fried chicken, mashed potatoes and French style green beans.

They spoke about each other's day during dinner.

Dinner was finished off with warm apple pie topped with vanilla ice cream.

Delicious, they all enjoyed the conversation and scrumptious meal.

It was a deep sleep.

Joseph woke up with a huge smile on his face.

Reminiscing about his parents lovingly that were long gone.

Ah, beautiful memories.

He wished he could sleep a little longer and perhaps continue the same dream.

Back to work.

He'll always remember that fond dream with glee and love.

Great memories not to be forgotten.

As he walked to public transportation, he could not hide his smile.

Still, he misses his Mom and Pop.

He will always keep them in his heart and fond memories.

Until they meet again.

Joseph was a great son and his parents appreciated it.

Just as in his workplace, his love for work is appreciated by his colleagues and superiors.

Another day awaits him, and he looks forward to it.

Joseph, a good man indeed.

HOPE, FAITH and CHARITY

Life is very mysterious and unpredictable.

Life is wonderful.

There will be moments in our lifetime,

where will be experience happiness and joy.

Other times, trials and tribulations.

When that gloomy cloud of desperation and sadness grips you,

do not lose faith.

The Universe, God in all his/her manifestations are with you and will provide resolution and consolation.

It's seems easy to say, but that is the truth.

Continue life and be proactive as you must use your strength to overcome.

Your actions and faith will help you through anything.

Nothing is impossible.

Faith and hope will pull you through.

Charity.

Ah, yes, charity.

Take a moment out of your time to help your brethren.

Family and friends.

This action of charity will bring you happiness, a sense of wellbeing.

Your act of charity will bring joy to your heart and to those who received it.

Faith Hope and Charity.

All three go hand in hand.

Your life will be filled of joyous fulfillment.

Do good and it will be reciprocated by God and the Universe.

Alas, give from your heart without expecting reciprocation.

It will bring you peace.

Faith Hope and Charity.

FIVE KNIVES

It was a difficult time for the Lambert family.

Just one week ago, the loving father, Robert Lambert passed away unexpectedly.

He died in his sleep, according to medical authorities, of natural causes.

No one expected this, especially his children.

He had two hard working sons, Dior and Christian.

Their mother died when they were very young.

Robert raised them as an only parent.

Since he had to work, he hired a nanny named Claire.

She was wonderful with both children.

Smothered them with love.

Robert gave his sons all his love and attention.

Ensured that they were well behaved and encouraged them to seek a higher education.

They did.

Dior was an English professor and Christian an attorney.

They both made their father proud.

He attended their graduations with great pride.

Tears welled up in his eyes as their names were announced during graduation.

Robert did all he could do to raise and influence to be young men with good values.

Dior and Christian moved to different states upon graduation to pursue their careers.

They maintained constant contact with their dad and visited him often.

Robert kept a secret from them, the only secret he never confided in them.

He did not want to hurt nor burden his children with his tribulations.

Robert had five friends, or so called "close friends" during his lifetime.

Unfortunately, these five close friends betrayed him in many ways.

The friends did things that were unforgivable.

They figuratively stabbed him in the back.

He found that he could not forgive them and removed them from his life.

Friends, especially close friends would never betray another as they did.

Robert bought five classic cooking knives at a cutlery store.

He took these knives to a hardware store to have them each engraved with the full names of those that betrayed him.

It was a symbolic powerful gesture.

These five knives served to remind him that not all friends are true and loyal.

He kept these knives safely stored in a dresser draw in his bedroom.

Every once in a while, he would look at the knives to remind him to not trust all.

All that glitters is not gold.

Although Christian and Dior never saw the knives, their father taught this lesson to them so that they may not experience what he did in life.

When Robert died, many family members and friends attended the wake at the funeral parlor.

Those five close friends were aware of Robert's death and attended.

They were full of remorse, but it was too late to say, "I'm sorry".

Neither of the children knew who the betrayers were, therefore greeted them as they did the others that attended.

With grace and gratefulness.

Within a week, Dior went to his late father's house to clean up and put the house up for sale.

He threw away clothes, donated furniture to the Salvation Army, but shared some memorable keepsakes with his brother, Christian.

As Dior went into his father's bedroom, he came upon the dresser draws.

Their laid the five engraved knives.

He recognized the names.

Dior immediately contacted his brother and told him of what he found.

They were puzzled.

At the funeral parlor, the names engraved on the knives were in the memorial attendee book.

Dior and Christian contacted the five "friends" and met scheduled to meet them in person.

They told him that their father left them gifts.

Within a month, the meeting was scheduled, and they met for lunch at a nice local restaurant.

Beforehand, Dior and Christian wrapped up the knives and neatly wrapped them up in red gift boxes.

After finishing lunch, while at the table, Robert's children gave the friends the gift boxes and asked them to open them there in their presence.

They did.

Those five friends became very emotional and choked up.

Both sons looked at each other, shook hands with their father's "friends" and departed.

The knives would forever remind Lambert's friends how they stabbed him in the back.

The five knives.

FRIENDS FOREVER

Sincere friendship, that is what we all wish for.

Not just sincere, but loving relationships that will last until our final

goodbyes in life.

There are people that believe that some friendships are transitory.

That may be the case, but I'd rather not think of that at the present

tense.

The friendship I offer is truly sincere with love.

A friendship that I wish can be forever.

It really does take two to tango, the other friend may not feel the same

way as I do.

We spend time together laughing, joking and get down to the nitty

gritty about life in general.

Then the wheels of time inevitably turn for many.

The separation of the true friendship we believed, is changed because

of different factors.

Educational and professional pursuits.

The creation and importance to some of family over friendship.

New friendships formed with others that may have more in common than with you.

That's one of the sad parts.

A friend departing your side to enrich a new friendship.

You ask yourself why not integrate and nourish one special friend with the new one.

As much as you want to maintain that loving relationship, the other friend decides to depart from your side.

That's where the disillusion sets in.

Did I do something wrong to deserve the desertion from my friend or friends?

You question yourself.

A question which may not have a response.

You can only wish your friend the best in life and hope that your paths meet once again.

I've been fortunate to keep supportive, loving friends and I know that won't ever change.

I desire to have a fruitful friendship to old age until death do us part.

Even then, the memories of a good friend will remain alive in our heart and mind.

Never forget that good friend, that friend for life.

In the meantime, treasure the friends you have right here and now.

Bravo to long lasting friendships.

GODS DESCENDING

Norman was excited early that morning.

The weather was picture perfect.

Yes, picture perfect.

Sunny and comfortable temperatures.

He and his godchildren were invited to a religious and spiritual event by his good friend, a lovely lady initiated as a Priestess of Eleggua*.

Eleggua is the Orisha associated with the crossroads in life, playful yet serious and to be respected at all times.

The spiritual event was based on a centuries old spiritual and religious practice named Lukumi also know in Spanish as La Regla de Ocha.

This religion originated thousands of years from the continent of Africa.

A religion with a multitude of followers throughout the Caribbean and the United States.

The event took place in a nearby state from where Norman lived.

It was a long drive, but very much well worth it.

On the way, Norman and his godchildren chatted and caught up on their daily lives.

There was laughter in the car.

Little did they know what a special event it would be.

It was a homage given to the Orisha Chango, which has many attributes including from nature; lightning, thunderbolts and fire.

His attributes also include, dance, the power of the tongue, divine justice and royalty.

The King of Kings within the pantheon of the Orishas.

The lovely lady, Priestess of Eleggua, was doing this to appease her godfather's tutelary Orisha Chango.

This event took place in a large barn style type of house.

The house was painted a light to medium grey, a beautiful house indeed.

Approximately, one hundred people attended this event.

Olorishas, Aleyos and Aborishas.

Olorishas are initiated Priests, Aleyos devotees to La Regla de Ocha and Aborishas, those that have undergone the initial initiations into the beautiful religion of Santeria. La Regla de Ocha.

One of the protocols when attending such a gathering is to dress in white if possible.

Upon entering the home, Norman and his godchildren saw a sea of white.

People dressed in their finest white clothes, similar dressing your best when attending a Sunday Catholic mass at Church.

White within the religion, represents humility and peace.

The energy was very strong within the home, positive and full of peace.

There were elders and young folks alike. greeting each other with sincere smiles and love.

A sight to be felt and seen.

Very welcoming to outsiders and those initiated.

The intent of this beautiful event was to not only pay homage to Chango but to invoke his very presence.

This type of event hired seasoned drummers and a singer also known in Lukumi as an Akpon who knew how to bring the Orishas to earth.

They knew the type of drumming and singing to appease the Orishas and invoke their presence amongst all who that attended.

The drumming and singing started in the early afternoon.

Everyone was respectful towards each other.

The majority knew the songs and sang the chorus along with the Akpon.

As the singing and drumming started, the ambiance in the home began to change.

A strong energy full of peace, heat and coolness which made your hairs stand up on end.

The drummers played the set of drums named Anya strongly and the Akpon started calling upon the Orishas with strength and faith.

It didn't take very long for the Orishas to make their presence known.

The skies outside of the home brightened up and those with an intuitive eye could see a multitude of bright colorful rays descending from the heavens and penetrating the roof and ceiling of the house.

White, Red, Yellow, Blue and an array of other beautiful colors.

The rays came down with an energetic force spiritually affecting both the initiated and non-initiated attendees.

The Priest of Chango who was dancing to the same Orisha, went into a deep trance.

Mimicking the attributes of this beautiful Orisha.

The attributes of this Orisha full of divine energy touched many of the invitees.

Chango, through the trance of the Priest, made his entrance through full trance into the home.

It was a joyful experience for all to see, all praising and thanking Chango for visiting earth from the heavens.

As the drummers continued playing and singing, other Orishas started their voyage from the heavens to earth and benevolently possessed the bodies and minds of the Priests that praised them.

Chango.

Yemaya.

Ochun.

Obatala.

Oya.

Agayu.

BabaluAye/ObaluAye.

Gods descending.

The air on the first floor of the home, felt electric.

Full of energy that the Orishas brought along with them.

In this particular event, the Orishas spoke in English and Spanish, but above all based on the ancient African Yoruba language.

Lukumi was spoken by these beautiful Orishas.

Their intent was to bring messages from the highest in the heavens known as Olodumare, the supreme God known in the Lukumi spirituality and religion.

The messages were advice given to those that sought divine consult, resolution to their tribulations, problems and healing; both physically and spiritually.

This came from the Orishas that honored all those in their presence.

What a lovely day indeed!

The divinities intermingling with human beings.

Many of the attendees were affected emotionally as the advice given to them by the Orisha was so accurate.

Prophecy and advice unbeknownst from the human vessels, the Priests and Priestesses that did not know beforehand the afflictions affecting the attendees.

It was magical.

Divine.

The Orishas that came to visit were visibly happy to be present amongst the human beings attending.

Divine interaction.

Gods and Goddesses present and mingling with the attendees of this homage to Chango.

Those present, respectfully greeted the divine in their very presence.

A lovely site to see and be remembered.

The Orishas were present for a limited time, perhaps a few hours.

They were there to see the human beings.

To give advice.

To provide healing.

To hear their pleas.

Once they heard their pleas, the divine deities delivered them directly to the Almighty Olodumare for resolution.

All was heard by Olodumare.

Once the spiritual event ended, delicious food was served to all attendees.

Food, drink, productive conversation and love shared.

Gifts were given to all as gratitude for attending this drumming.

Many took home fruits that were placed in the royal and sacred throne dedicated to Chango.

The fruits were considered blessed as they were laid in front of the shrine to Chango.

Fruits to be eaten or to be used by the invitees to clean themselves of all negativity.

The event was successful.

There was peace, love and unity amongst all present.

This was a special event for the divine and human beings to interact with one another.

Maferefun Orisha.

Praise to all Orisha.

Gods descended to see, hear and speak.

Gods descending.

HE HATES

The noun hate was never a word used in his vocabulary.

He despised the word, as it made him very uncomfortable.

He may have used disliked, but never hate.

But then that terrible disease, out of the blue, affected his most loved one.

His mother.

He didn't hate his mother, rather, adored her.

But he hated the disease afflicting her.

He never fathomed what was to come into their lives.

There are no riddles here.

Dementia.

The disease is dementia.

Dementia.

His mother was the most nourishing, affectionate, loving person any son or daughter could have.

She gave her all, her love, her soul to her children.

She was very protective as well.

They were the apple in her eyes.

She was beautiful, both inside and out.

Always poised, polite, a woman of great strength.

She was and still is very pretty, no matter how time has gone by.

Yet, for the most part, her rational mind is not there any longer.

She has her good days where she can converse with her son,

then the bad days where she is aggressive and at times displays violent, aggressive behavior.

That latter was not a trait she displayed when she was well of mental health.

She is no longer an independent person.

Now she depends on assistance from professional caregivers and her son.

Due to this illness, the son has become her caregiver.

Although she is attended by a stranger that has become a family member,

his mother mainly relies on her son.

She calls him repeatedly as she lacks that trust from the professional caregiver.

The mother has other ailments which are, fortunately, under control.

Her son ensures, she takes her medication on time.

She has forgotten to swallow her medication with water and her son observes her to make sure, she takes her pills.

What we take for granted or not even think of, taking medication with a glass of water, is difficult for her.

Her appetite has diminished.

Paranoia sets in and she believes she is being poisoned by her son, either with food or medication.

Of course, it's normal for the son to be upset by this behavior.

The trust she once had in her son is gone.

There are times, she displays affection, an almost clear mind which her son loves.

She takes long naps during the day and wakes up confused, not knowing if it's day or night.

Dementia is such a cruel illness.

The worst part is that there is no scientific cure.

It is a progressive disease.

The son is not totally prepared for the future outcome of his mother.

In the meantime, he will continue to take loving care of his Mom and be as compassionate and loving as possible.

He hates the illness.

It's a cruel joke bestowed upon both mother and son.

All he can do is be there for her.

HE WAS ONLY 4 YEARS OLD

He was an innocent 4-year-old boy.

Full of joy.

Loved to dance.

Loved to make others laugh.

He loved to learn from his older brother.

His older brother was in 1st grade in school.

He looked up to his brother and appreciated all that his brother could teach him from school.

The 4-year-old boy with a vivid mind at times was an old soul.

In his limited vocabulary due to his age, he expressed himself beautifully and clearly.

He adored his parents and was well behaved.

The young boy had mumps and loved the homemade chocolate pudding his mother treated him to.

At times timid with strangers, but once he warmed up, he was a doll.

He had full cheeks and was beautiful.

His mother was very protective, although could not care for him 24 hours as she would like, as she had to work.

She left him in the hands of her younger brother, his uncle.

Little did the mother know, that the young uncle, under his care, would take away his innocence.

The abode where the family lived, was small.

The uncle slept in the same bedroom as the young innocent boy along with his brother.

His family member, the uncle took advantage of night and day to sexually assault such an innocent boy.

The uncle told the young boy that it was okay and that he must never tell his mother of the "love making".

The uncle was very careful to clean up the young boy in the bathroom after "raping" him.

It was incest, in the worst possible way.

The young boy did not enjoy the "love making" or as the uncle would say the "I love you" words he said to the innocent boy.

The boy was in pain but could not speak about his experience to any family members.

He suffered in silence.

If his mother knew of what happened, she would have ostracized her brother or even worse, violence.

The young boy became a man and never spoke of his experience as a child to his family.

He felt ashamed.

Alas, he forgave his uncle in silence.

He never blamed his mother as she thought he was in the safe hands of her brother.

In adulthood, the uncle became very sick, and the once young boy cared for him.

He forgave him but never forgot his childhood experience.

The young 4-year-old boy turned adult became the better man.

He was only 4 years old.

Innocent and not protected.

His uncle eventually transitioned, and the once 4-year-old boy only wished him peace and love.

I PRAY

I pray for forgiveness.

I pray for divine enlightenment.

I pray for world peace and the end of war.

I pray for those in need.

I pray to be a better person.

I pray to recognize my mistakes and correct them.

I pray for my friends and family.

I pray for those that are ill.

I pray that I see overlook faults in others,

and instead praise them for their virtues.

I pray that world leaders be enlightened and seek peace instead of war.

I pray that science find cures for all illness that befall mankind.

I pray for a better environment for our future generations.

I pray that we replace hate with love.

I pray for tolerance and understanding of one another.

I pray that one day I can be a positive influence on others.

I pray my words are sweetened with honey and are never bitter.

I pray that I can be exemplary demonstrating love, so that others may follow suit.

I pray for the end of world hunger.

I pray for parents to be positive role models in their children's lives.

I pray that everyone is treated equal.

I pray for those that suffer drug addiction and seek help.

I pray that we respect each other's religions and spiritual beliefs.

I pray for the elderly.

I pray for our children.

I pray for the dearly departed.

I pray for the infirmed that are in hospitals and other medical institutions.

I pray that everyone has hope for a better tomorrow.

I pray that everyone has a roof over their heads.

I pray for the homeless.

I pray for the survival of this world.

I pray that you pray with me.

I pray for myself.

I pray that my words are heard by the Universe.

I pray that I breathe prayer day and night.

I pray for love throughout the world.

I pray that I continue to pray for the benefit of us all.

I pray.

I pray.

I pray.

INSEPARABLE FRIENDS

It was a perfect sunny day.

Angelo and Carlos planned to hang out and spend time with each other.

Their friendship spanned over two decades.

They were not only friends; it was more of a brotherly love.

This type of relationship is hard to come by.

It was a spontaneous plan to meet.

They spent hours together, reminiscing about the years they enjoyed with each other.

It was a carefree day they spent together.

They walked miles, laughing and joking around.

Decided to have a scrumptious lunch in a historic neighborhood of New York City.

It was a sunny hot day.

Carlos, seeking the shade on the sunny sidewalk.

Angelo loved the sun as humid as it was.

They decided to have a scrumptious lunch at one of the popular Italian restaurants in the neighborhood.

The food was delicious, albeit the service was a bit slow.

They caught up on their daily lives as they had not seen each other in a while.

The encounter was amusing.

They wanted to meet up as Angelo was taking a mini vacation in the next few days.

As they caught up on their lives, Carlos was slightly sad and felt a bit melancholic that Angelo would be away from town for several weeks.

When they left the restaurant, they took a long walk and decided to go shopping.

Suddenly, the heavens, which was unexpected, opened up.

It started to pour heavy cool rain.

They didn't carry umbrellas as the weatherman,

did not correctly get the weather correctly.

The forecast was way off.

Mother Nature had tricks up her sleeve.

Nonetheless, the cooling rain was welcome by the two friends.

There clothes were soaked, and they did not care.

It was a fun day, regardless of the unexpected weather pattern.

The sun appeared once again, and their clothes air dried.

It was a fantastic day.

Lunch and unexpected weather.

It was a fun and memorable day.

INVISIBLE FACE

Dr. Travis is a renowned psychologist living and working in Beverley Hills, California.

His patients are very wealthy and come from throughout the United States seeking therapy.

The crème of the crème.

He takes his work very seriously and is very talented in treating his patients.

Providing counsel, constructive advice and comfort.

Some of his patients have been seeing him for years.

His voice is so comforting, that they just make appointments to hear the soothing sound coming from his throat.

It's almost magical to them.

No, he is not a hypnotist, he is a board certified therapist licensed in various states.

There are some patients that fly him from California to their state of residence for counseling.

He is that good!

There is once specific patient which he found fascinating and troubling.

This patient is a very successful defense attorney living in the suburbs of Beverly Hills.

A secret to all, only confided to Dr. Travis, is that he believes he is an invisible man.

A mental illness, perhaps a bipolar type of disorder.

He tells Dr. Travis that at times, he is in the courthouse representing a client, and believes the judge and other staff do not see him.

Although they greet him, he does not hear them.

Dr. Travis counsels this patient trying to help him understand or discover why he feels that way.

It has taken many clinical sessions to help him.

Although this relationship between patient and Dr. Travis is professional, recently it has affected Dr. Travis in an unusual manner.

One morning, the psychologist went about his usual chores during the morning prior to going to his office.

He went to the kitchen to brew a cup of fresh delicious Colombian coffee.

While sipping the coffee at the kitchen counter, he had an eerie feeling.

He touched his unshaven face, feeling the hair that had to be taken care of before leaving his home.

He was a very well-polished man.

Once he finished his coffee, he went to his beautiful white tiled bathroom.

He looked in the mirror to brush his teeth, shave, and then shower.

Dr. Travis, strangely, could not see his face.

He could feel it but not see it.

He started to tremble; he was frightened.

Anyone would!

He could see his physical body below the face, but the head was not visible.

Dr. Travis ran out of the bathroom into his bedroom and laid down.

Trying to compose himself and convince his mind that it was an illusion he saw.

It wasn't real he thought.

Once he composed himself, he reentered the bathroom.

Again, no head, no face, just the rest of his body.

Due to this scary incident, he decided not to shave.

He closed his eyes and fortunately felt his face.

Washed his face and dried it with the nearby bath towel.

He returned to the mirror and the same, the face was not visible at all.

He panicked.

Dr. Travis decided not to go to the office and cancelled all his appointments.

Once again, laying in bed, he tried his best to decipher why he was going through awful experience.

He called no one as he did not want to be labeled "crazy".

Dr. Travis continued to think while laying in his bed why this was occurring.

He had an "aha!" moment.

His "invisible" patient's condition somehow was psychologically affecting him, subconsciously contagious.

He took his patient's condition to heart and mind and affected him deeply.

Meditation and breathing exercises were a tool he used frequently to cleanse his mind of the problems that his patients discussed with him.

A cleansing exercise to be refreshed.

He sat up on his comfortable bed and breathed.

Breathed deeply.

Allowing himself to realize what he experienced was not real at all.

He breathed so deep, about ten minutes that he experienced lightheadedness.

Dr. Travis decided to take a therapeutic nap to help him.

Naps are very refreshing!

Once he woke up, he went to the bathroom.

Preparing to look in the mirror, he took a deep breath.

He saw his face once again.

It was visible.

Dr. Travis was thrilled.

He realized that his patient affected him deeply and that he must create a mental shield between him and the patient.

We all learn from our experiences.

He learned his lesson to not take his patients troubles personally.

He had to prepare, this patient with the invisible face would seem him in two days.

Shield and protect.

He hopes that he will not experience the same with the patient.

KARLA

Karla had a peaceful sleep during the night.

Unfortunately, she woke up confused.

She did not recognize that she was home.

Did not recognize her surroundings.

Her bedroom.

Her perfumes.

She thought she was in someone else's home.

Karla asked her beloved daughter where her children were.

She did not recognize her daughter.

Confusion.

A daytime "nightmare.".

Her daughter, Carleen was distressed by this condition and did not know what to do.

Carleen could only sit by her mother's bedside and console her.

It took at least an hour for Karla to realize that she was at home.

The awful episode was horrific for both.

Patience and compassion were indeed needed.

Carleen consoled her mother to calm her.

She spoke to her mother, recalling and conversing the past and present.

Karla finally came to her senses, return of sanity.

She finally came to her senses and realized that she was in her beautiful home filled with peace and love.

This was not the

 first time Karla experienced confusion.

Carleen, understanding her mother's

bad and god days.

Compassion, and love was all Carleen could offer her mother.

Peace of mind and not allow these episodes her mother was Carleen would affect her sanity.

Carleen prays for this condition to eventually dissipate.

May this condition through medical and divine intervene heal the mind of Karla.

That is Karleen's wish, for her mother to be healed both physically and spiritually.

May this be so.

LETTING GO

It's only a matter of time.

As the hands of the clock move forward, they await.

The long-gone spirits of his ancestors call out to him.

"Enough", they say, enough suffering in this mundane planet Earth.

Their outstretched comforting arms,

promising a better tomorrow in their heavenly existence.

"Come", they declare.

"We will wait for you patiently. When you are ready and say yes, we will embrace you with love and peace".

There will be no more pain, no more suffering.

You fought a good fight.

It may be today.

It may be tomorrow.

Say your goodbyes to your closest loved ones, as they intuitively know the time is near.

When the appropriate time arrives, let go without fear.

Do not be afraid.

A change from one existing plane to another.

Allow the shackles holding you down on Earth to unlock.

You will be free again.

No more pain.

No more anguish of mind and body.

The inevitable is near.

You ancestors welcome you with peace and love.

Goodbye my dear.

It's ok to let go, your family and friends are prepared as can be.

They do not want you to suffer.

Adiós mi amor. Aurevoir mon amour.

LIFE IS PECULIAR

Life can throw speed balls,

in a fast and furious manner.

These can be overwhelming, leaves us breathing heavily,

sweating, short of breath.

We wonder, why me?

We try to analyze these experiences and at the very moment of the speedball,

can't find the answer or the reason.

We pray or meditate for enlightenment.

A hint may or not be revealed.

The overwhelming desire to find the "why" can be frustrating.

Then, sooner, and hopefully sooner than later, the aha moment

appears.

The solution to our present issue is gifted to us out of thin air.

Like pulling a rabbit out of a magician's hat.

Yes, life is full of both good and not so good surprises, yet,

we survive.

So, when these curve balls, speed balls, life's challenges hit us,

know that it is temporary, and a solution will appear.

Life is good.

Have faith and move forward.

Life is marvelous and full of surprises.

I think of life as a beautiful rose with the inevitable thorns that grown on the stem.

There are no precise adjectives that I can use to emphasize that life is great.

Life is full of love, peace, joie de vivre, and all peculiar things.

Enjoy life!

LA VIDA ES PECULIAR

La Vida puede lanzar bolas de velocidad,

de una manera rápida y furiosa.

Estos pueden ser abrumadores, nos deja respirando pesadamente,

sudoración, falta de aliento.

Nos preguntamos, ¿por qué yo?

Tratamos de analizar estas experiencias y en el momento mismo de la bola rápida,

No Podemos encontrar la respuesta o la razón.

Oramos o meditamos pidiendo iluminación.

Una pista puede o no ser revelada.

El abrumador deseo de encontrar el "por qué" puede ser frustrante.

Entonces, más pronto, y ojalá más pronto que tarde, el momento aja

Aparece.

La solución a nuestro problema actual nos ha sido otorgada de la nada.

Como sacar un conejo del sombrero de un mago.

Sí, la vida está llena de sorpresas buenas y no tan buenas, sin embargo,

nosotros sobrevivimos

Entonces, cuando estas bolas curvas, bolas de velocidad, los desafíos de la vida nos golpean,

sepan que es temporal, y aparecerá una solución.

La vida es buena.

Ten fe y sigue adelante.

La vida es maravillosa y llena de sorpresas.

Pienso en la vida como una hermosa rosa con las inevitables espinas que crecen en el tallo.

No hay adjetivos precisos que pueda usar para enfatizar que la vida es excelente.

La vida está llena de amor, paz, alegría de vivir y todas las cosas peculiares.

¡Disfruta la vida!

LIVING IN THE STREETS

Lucius is a very observant young man.

As he walked and shopped in Spanish Harlem, he watched.

People of all colors walking in the streets.

People living in the streets.

He walked along 110th Street to 116th Street.

Exploring from 2nd Avenue to Park Avenue.

People walking in the streets.

Living in the streets.

He observed their stature

The perceived beauty.

The perceived ugliness.

Their clothing.

Their desperation.

Some with smiles, others with frozen expressions on their faces.

Living in the streets.

Lucius wondered about their thoughts as they walked or stood still in the streets.

The man that smiled at him with butterfly stitches on his forehead and bloodshot eye.

The man was walking in the street.

It was cold outside.

Lucius stopped for a moment to light a cigarette.

He was approached timidly by the same man, asking for a few coins to get a bite to eat.

Lucius kindly obliged and gave him two quarters.

The man asked if he could get a few drags from the cigarette that Lucius was smoking.

Lucius smile at him and offered him a cigarette.

The man was appreciative and smiled once more.

Lucius wondered about this man.

The man's life story, his history, his current situation and what future awaits him.

Living in the street.

Lucius finished his cigarette and stepped on it in the street.

He continued his walk in this colorful part of Manhattan.

Lucius noticed who were the residents in this part of town and the outsiders including tourists.

The tourists looking at their handheld maps seeking direction.

After a couple of hours walking around Spanish Harlem, he headed to the subway to go back home.

He enjoyed his walk and was fascinated with all he saw and people he encountered.

At the next corner was the train station.

Downtown number 6 train.

He quickly swiped his Metrocard at the subway turnstile.

Lucius made it on time to board the train that was arriving on the subway platform.

More people to observe on the fully packed train.

This train ride will inundate Lucius' mind even more.

Let the fun begin.

MARY'S LIFE

Mary woke up somewhat confused.

She was hungry and afraid that there was nothing to eat at home.

Before going to the bathroom to wash her face and brush her teeth,

she headed swiftly to the kitchen.

Mary quickly opened doors of the kitchen pantry and cupboard draws to see if there was food.

She was relieved to know that there was food.

This was not the first time she awoke with these strange thoughts.

Fear of hunger and no money to buy food.

After seeing that there was plentiful food,

she felt comfort, a sense of relief.

Mary went to the bathroom, brushed her teeth and took a warm comforting shower.

The thought of not having food readily available to her was still embedded in her mind.

After the shower, she dressed in a pair of comfortable black slacks, a loose white cotton blouse and stylish black leather shoes.

Shortly thereafter, she prepared a bountiful and healthy breakfast.

Two slices of buttered whole wheat toast, with strawberry jam and a medium sized bowl of delicious oatmeal.

She was satisfied with her meal.

Her tummy full.

Feeling confident that she had at least that one meal for the day.

After washing the dishes and utensils, the thought of poverty and lack of food entered her mind.

She once again, to reassure herself, checked the pantry and cupboards again.

There was food.

Mary had a healthy weight and always took good care of her appearance in public.

Perhaps the thought of hunger and lack of food derived from her childhood.

This is Mary's life.

When growing up as a child, her parents lacked money at times as it was during the depression era of the 1930's.

Money to buy food was scarce.

Therefore, the family ate food only once a day.

They went to bed with hungry stomachs and worried minds.

Her mother Martha worked as a maid with a wealthy family and her father, Stanley, a metal worker at a factory.

The factory where Stanley worked closed down due to the economy.

Her mother's work hours as a maid were reduced to half.

The financial income came solely from Martha working as a part time maid.

Many people during the depression era suffered the outcome that Mary and family experienced.

Lack of money and food.

Some folks begged in the streets or discreetly stole food from the local food markets.

Mary's childhood experiences reflect her fears of today.

Those experiences never left her.

Fortunately, Mary was able to complete her studies in a public high school and graduated.

She swore she would not allow her childhood experience to affect her future.

Mary went on to study secretarial studies.

Secretarial studies were very common for young ladies.

She found a job as a secretary at a law firm.

She only spent money from her salary as needed.

The money left over she hid under her mattress for a "rainy day".

She accumulated large amounts of money.

Finally, she found a bank that fell under the regulations and laws of the Federal Deposit Insurance Corporation (FDIC) which was established in 1933.

This offered protection to her finances.

She deposited the money accumulated in a FDIC regulated bank located in her neighborhood.

Mary decided that if she married a young man, she would never have children.

She did not want her children to suffer what she did as a child.

Eventually she married a young handsome man named Thomas.

Interestingly enough, he also suffered the same childhood as she did.

He also agreed not to have children.

They married and lived humble lives.

Humble, but happy.

They were a bit of penny pinchers but nonetheless they found ways of enjoying their life without spending too much money.

They visited free museums, art exhibits and also music concerts that were free of charge.

Sometimes they treated themselves to movie theaters.

They traveled by car to their mini vacation destinations.

Ten years into their loving marriage, Thomas fell ill and diagnosed with late stage prostate cancer.

Physicians tried their best to treat him, but the cancer was discovered too late.

Within two months, Thomas passed away.

Devastation overwhelmed Mary.

She was left alone and felt lonely.

Mary continued working until she was old enough to retire.

She remained in the same apartment which was rent controlled.

She had few friends and was reclusive.

History repeated itself again as Mary's mother was widowed at an early age.

The fear of poverty and hunger continued to haunt her.

Seeing a psychologist or psychiatrist was not an option for her.

Being under the care of mental health professionals was a stigma to those treated.

She dealt with her fears as best as she could.

Religion, after her husband's death helped her greatly with mourning and grieving.

The parish at the church she attended were very supportive.

Mary died at the age of eighty nine.

Ironically, she did not die poor.

In her living will, she donated all the money she saved to a charitable organization for the poor.

This was Mary's life.

MY HEART WEEPS

At this late hour, on August 4, 2019, I share the below with you.

It's not poem or prose.

I've been catching up on the national news and totally dismayed, perturbed.

Domestic and International terrorism.

Hate crimes due to the color of our skin, spiritual beliefs, sexual orientation and an array of issues.

Simply put; racism, misogyny, genderphobia, homophobia et al.

My heart weeps deeply.

My soul is in turmoil and overwhelmed.

Our very own humanity is divisive, full of hate.

Not all, but much of humanity.

Since this may have not affected us personally, we turn a blind eye.

I beseech that you don't turn a blind eye, ACT!

Here in the United States of America, the Occupant of the White House refuses to call these hate crimes.

I ask that you write to him and his administration.

Contact your local congressional leaders.

Let your voice be heard and state that you will not stand for this madness.

Your voice, your written word is very powerful.

Utilize it!

Make a difference.

If you do not know your legislators, google it.

Make a difference in this world we live in.

You can do it.

I can do it.

Be heard.

Excuse my "French", but all these deaths, gun shootings are not acceptable. #GTFOH

Rise and make a difference!

You never know if this may affect you personally today or in the future.

Let it not happen again.

2020 is right around the corner, get those MF's out of office if they do not represent your morals and values.

Lastly, I ask you to share my post or copy and paste.

Peace, love and light to all.

MY OKAN ANI

In the southern west of Nigeria, there is one of the beautiful largest ethnic groups named Yoruba.

In the Yoruba language, Okan Ani, is defined as two hearts that beats as one.

My friend, you are my Oka Ani.

It is known that children of the deities Elegba and Chango, are Okan Ani.

I'm a child of Elegba, and you, a child of Chango.

You are truly my Okan Ani.

Interestingly enough, you and I met through a loveable friend.

Our friendship began since then.

You and I communicated frequently via various types of communication to catch up on our lives.

We clowned around.

We spoke about Orisha and Egun worship.

We spoke about our daily lives as well.

So many laughs that were cherished by both.

Unbeknownst to me, perhaps not to worry me, you were diagnosed with a terminal illness.

You kept that to yourself as not to have others worry about you.

Determined, you fought this illness as best as you could.

You were always a trooper.

Always setting challenging goals to reach.

You did.

I wish I knew your turmoil, so that I could be by your side, understandably, you kept it amongst your family members and very close friends.

I loved you as you are.

Although a male, you were a fabulous Diva.

Charismatic.

Attracting people when you entered a room.

Magical, friendly and sociable.

You were the sparkling ball of all soirees.

Ensuring everyone had a laugh with you.

During the past couple of years, you kept that secret of illness to yourself.

Understandably so.

Iku, death, was very close to you.

I wish there was something I can do spiritually to heal you through divine intervention.

I'm proud that you fought as much as you could to conquer illness.

You were always feisty and strong.

Children of Chango, have that admirable characteristic.

To conquer and be victorious.

Unfortunately, this awful terminal illness engulfed your body.

Not your heart, not your mind, but, your physical body.

Today, your body was weak of all the fighting, although your mind was to conquer.

Your body ceded to this horrible and unrelenting illness.

You are in the celestial heavens now.

A beautiful angel on earth and now in the heavens.

Oh boy, the gates of heaven welcome you.

Your bright smile, sense of humor and fabulous Diva presence.

I imagined that your angel wings are sparkling with all the colors of the rainbow.

A bright angel left earth and heaven honored to have you amongst celestial beings.

My Okan, heart, is heavy, but you are in a better place.

No more pain or anguish.

You are whole above with wings.

You will be missed by your family and friends.

A circle of friends which are innumerable.

You touched many lives and will be remembered.

I surely will.

I bid you farewell.

My Okan Ani.

I will miss you immensely.

Until we meet again.

My Okan Ani.

PECULIAR REALISTIC DREAMS

It was a busy day for Preston.

He ran errands endlessly to prepare for the following day.

Ensuring that it would be a perfect gathering of friends and family.

He ran into friends on the street, friendly greetings and brief conversations as not to be rude.

Preston's shopping seemed endless, but he was able to get everything done.

Alas, he arrived at his cozy home and took a breather.

Upon arriving he took a calming breath and had a cool glass of water.

He sat down on his favorite cozy chair in his bedroom and pondered about his day's activities.

Preston changed to comfortable lounge pants and a favorite t-shirt.

He thought about his day and relaxed.

It was too late to cook dinner, therefore, ordered takeout food.

Italian food to be exact.

Isn't it great to have delicious food delivered to your door?

One of his favorite dishes, Spaghetti Carbonara accompanied by a glass of his favorite red wine he had at home.

A simple dish, yet very satisfying.

It was a tiring day but very amusing once he thought about it.

After eating, Preston decided to take a quick nap.

He dreamt about his outing and unrelated peculiar things, such as the trees and gardens he saw, he hadn't consciously noticed as he ran his errands.

Once he awoke from his nap, a long one at that, he prepared to shower and relax further.

He looks in his bathroom mirror and smiled.

Preston's mission accomplished for the day.

He took a long soothing share with his favorite body wash and allowed the pulsating water to massage his entire body.

It was relaxing to say the least.

Once he dried himself with the comfy towel, he dressed in comfortable pajamas.

He walked to the kitchen to make a fresh pot of espresso coffee, just enough for three cups, otherwise, he'd not be able to sleep at bedtime.

Along with the coffee, he ate a small meal, a Cesar chicken salad with enough dressing.

After completing his satisfying meal, Preston, went to the living room to catch up on local and world news.

He always wanted to be informed of the current events of the world.

After a few hours, he was tired and decided to call it a night.

The fresh linens on his queen size bed were inviting and waiting for him.

He quickly fell into a deep sleep.

What was most unusual is that he experienced life like dreams of dreams within dreams itself.

One dream created another, followed by another in his sleep.

His last dream was of a human character with peculiar facial features.

An impactful expression not to be forgotten.

He wasn't frightened during the dream state but came to the realization that the face somehow resembled a penguin face.

A penguin's face.

How strange is that?

When he awoke in the morning, he could still remember that penguin face.

Preston wasn't sure what to make of it, but it remained in his mind throughout the day.

Dreams can be peculiar, at times recalling things from our subconscious.

An attractive face with subtle penguin features.

The symbolism of that face was fascinating but unsure what it meant.

The dreams within the dreams stayed with him for quiet sometime.

Time to drink delicious coffee and get that uplift for his upcoming gathering.

RED BEAUTIFUL BUBBLES

It was a beautiful warm autumn day.

The inseparable friends, Cosmas and Damien made plans to meet for lunch and run errands locally.

They met at a local Italian restaurant that was very popular.

The restaurant was well known for their delicious food,

but also known for their slow service.

The restaurant was always packed.

They patiently waited for their lunch platters.

Both had a very good sense of humor.

Over lunch, they caught up on their daily lives as they had not seen each other for some time.

Cosmas and Damian conversed and had bouts of laughter over their recent experiences.

This was always occurred when they met.

They were so close that they were almost like blood brothers.

Their love for one each other was evident.

Once they had the scrumptious lunch, they shared a delectable Italian pastry accompanied by an expresso.

Cosmas and Damian were in no rush as they were having such a good time.

Once they left the restaurant, they walked the tree lined streets slowly and continuing their laughter.

They passed by beautiful homes and gardens and were in awe.

Although autumn, flowers were still blooming.

It was a sunny warm day.

Cosmas wished he brought along his sunglasses as the sun was brilliantly shining.

While they both talked and laughed, Cosmas saw bubbles in thin air.

Red beautiful transparent bubbles.

These were the type of bubbles children played with the soap bottles and small handle to blow colorful bubbles.

Many of us as children, enjoyed the bottled soap bubbles.

What was most peculiar during their walk, Cosmas saw the same bubbles flowing in the air towards him.

They were transparent but had a red transparent hue.

The bubbles would land on his face, it was very playful.

Some landed on his arms and burst.

The bubbles that burst had a cool refreshing feel on his arms.

Unusual, as there were no children nearby playing with bubbles.

They appeared from thin air.

Red beautiful bubbles.

Damian, for some reason or another did not see these bubbles.

They were only visible to Cosmos.

There was some meaning to this for Cosmos, but at the moment, he could not figure it out.

Perhaps, it was to bring out the inner child in him to bring joy and happiness.

Something he had not experienced in a long time.

Cosmos asked Damien if he saw the beautiful red transparent bubbles.

Damien, replied no.

He had no idea why Cosmos was experiencing this and went along with his perceived imagination.

Damien was happy that Cosmos "imagined" this as it made him happy.

Whatever made Cosmos happy, made Damien happy.

An unusual phenomenon from the heavens to bring joy to Cosmos.

The red to be deciphered at one time or another.

They continued their leisurely walk in the beautiful neighborhood and did not mention the incident again.

It was something to be accepted as is and not questioned.

Once they completed their promenade, they embraced like brothers and said goodbye to each other.

Both looked forward to seeing each other soon again.

It was a wonderful and fun day they would never forget.

Friendship and brotherly love which is rarely found.

May this beautiful relationship last for years to come.

REGINA

Beautiful Regina.

Experiencing trials and tribulations, she sought her friend and spiritual advisor.

She was in turmoil.

After many years of a long term relationship with her boyfriend, intuitively she felt he lied to her.

He was a player, not loyal.

He told her that he loved her, but actually, he did not.

Infidelity.

Lies.

Charming, but a manipulator.

He knew how to use his charm to enchant her.

Seven years wasted.

She loved him and trusted him.

He was unworthy of such trust.

Some men are like that, users.

Regina felt that she lost seven years of her life,

wasted, in a relationship that was all a lie.

As hard as it was, she had to swallow the hard pill that he would not change.

Valiantly, she decided to end the relationship.

Yes, it would be hard.

Better to end a relationship now, than to live a long time relationship with a liar.

Regina struggled with her decision.

Tears.

Broken hearted.

But she made the right decision.

She is intelligent, beautiful and deserves much better.

She deserves a man that will accept her as she is and love her like no other way.

A man that desires a long term relationship and grow old with love together.

Relationships are not perfect.

Yet, by compromising, bend a little, they can work out.

Regina, you deserve the best.

That Prince will manifest in your life.

Have patience and be open to a new love.

Wipe away the tears and open up your heart and mind.

Breathe deeply and allow the universe to bring this kind, loving man into your life.

Regina, you got this.

Her spiritual advisor told her she is worthy of so much more in life.

Regina, you will be victorious and fall head over heels when this prince arrives into your life.

Regina, happiness will once again manifest.

SCATHING SUMMER HEAT IN NYC

There is no escaping it.

It feels like ninety degrees Fahrenheit out in the street.

Perhaps 80 degrees with a seventy-humidity index.

Either, or, it is scathing outside.

Walking outside during these type of summer days is best to make it quick and fast.

The heat seems to cruelly rise from the city sidewalks.

Ideally, you can be in an inside pool, or near the ocean shore.

Perhaps by a cooling river.

Taking a nice dip in the cool waters, bringing your body temperature down.

Yes, cool refreshing waters.

Back in the day; in New York City, the young kids, even adults, would cool off with the fire hydrant sprinklers.

In the urban neighborhoods, also known as Johnny Pumps.

Those were the carefree days to soothe our bodies.

The boys and girls with t-shirts and shorts.

Whew, what great relief that brought.

The hot bright sunny sky would dry you off quickly.

Then back to the Johnny Pumps.

The joy of cooling off was accompanied by laughter and huge smiles.

Hell, no one wanted a heat stroke.

You had to do what you had to do.

What was that?

Seek alleviation from the scathing heat.

The bourgeois folks had their own methods, just as effective.

Air conditioners.

Ah, yes, the air conditioners at home.

Some were window a/c's, others had central air.

That accompanied by homemade, freshly squeezed lemon iced tea.

The not well to do, had Kool Aid pitchers of different flavors, just as refreshing as the above.

The heat did not discriminate.

It affected both poor and rich folks.

Of course, there were people that thoroughly enjoyed the heat, just as long they were well hydrated.

On the other hand, others that looked for the cooling temperatures, the shade on the other side of the city streets.

You can't beat the heat.

Summer is summer.

Some of us wonder how the hell folks deal with the scorching heat in the southern states or tropical islands.

I guess, they acclimate to it at an early age.

In New York City, when the people heard the music of the ice cream trucks, many know them as Mister Softee,

everyone ran out to buy the soothing treats.

Ice cream cones, chocolate or strawberry covered vanilla sundaes, orange cream popsicles.

Now, we can't forget the banana boats.

Remember those?

Three different flavored scoops of ice cream, a cold ripe banana drenched in strawberry or chocolate toppings.

Oh my, some of the toppings were butterscotch, old fashioned but delicious.

We can't forget the chocolate or rainbow sprinkles on these mouthwatering treats.

Yes, that's what we did on those scathing summer afternoons and nights.

Before I forget, many of us shared these treats with our siblings and friends.

Joked, laughed and made the best out of the summer.

Summers will always be immemorable.

Yes, even the harsh summer.

One thing to look forward to is the season of Autumn.

Just right around the corner.

SEEKING TRUE LOVE

He has just about everything in life he desires.

A great career, financial stability and a comfortable beautiful home.

Good health, wonderful friends and family that love and support him in his many endeavors.

He's traveled extensively for fun and business.

Through his travels he has visited beaches with crystalline waters and the warm beaming sunshine.

At times, touristy as he loves the arts.

Pools at resorts where he has been treated like a king.

Adventurous at tasting different foods throughout the world.

All these travel adventures have been with family, excellent friends and colleagues.

What else can he ask for?

Love.

True love.

Like fairy tales we read about during childhood.

The love that we have seen our parents display.

He is not looking for riches from another man or woman.

Not looking for codependency.

He wants true love.

Love that gives you that feeling of butterflies in your stomach.

Monogamy.

An amorous relationship, where you look into each other's eyes, and the love sparkles from within the soul.

He is not looking for a relationship just for the sake of companionship.

That would be settling for less than what he wants.

He wants love that makes him fly sky high filled with an indescribable happiness.

A long-lasting love that that makes the heart pitter patter when in each other's presence.

A partner that will hold hands in public and let other's see their love is palpable.

A lifelong partner, that will enjoy each other's company to the very end of their lives.

Yes, there will be some arguments and disagreements where they may not see eye to eye, but that is part of the relationship.

The best part of the latter is making up, laughing and kissing.

A fairytale?

No, this is possible.

Perhaps that love he seeks has passed and walked by him and not noticed.

Perhaps that love will come in a blink of an eye.

Yes, to love.

He is ready to meet that very special loving person.

The person that will accept both his virtues and faults, and vice versa.

May that day soon come.

He has hope and will hold on to that desire to love and be loved in return.

STEPHAN'S ENCOUNTER

It was 9PM.

Stephan was pouring his last cup of coffee for the night.

Suddenly, he felt the atmosphere change in the kitchen where he stood.

The air in the area became cool but very comfortable.

Intuitively, he knew there was a presence standing by him.

It was heavenly.

A feeling of love and peace.

God.

Stephan would daily pray to God.

Not for riches or wealth, he was humble.

All he prayed for was peace, good health and love for him and all loved ones.

He couldn't hear God's voice but knew He heard his prayers.

His faith was very strong.

He breathed God in and out, knowing he was beside him

This specific experience at 9pm in the kitchen was very different.

Stephan actually felt the presence of benevolence of the Almighty by his side.

He was overwhelmed, wrapped by God's presence.

What a wonderful feeling he felt.

Indescribable.

He opened his heart and mind to be inundated with this feeling of peace and love.

Stephan heard God's voice.

God telling him that he appreciated and loved the faith he always gave to him.

God told him he would never leave his side and that he would take care of him until the end of time.

A beautiful encounter between a human and the Divine.

Within a few minutes, the atmosphere room temperature returned to normal.

This was an encounter he would never forget.

He broke down to tears of joy.

An unexpected encounter with God.

Stephan will always remember as he praises Him.

If he could hug God, he would.

The prayers will be sufficient.

God is good, benevolent.

Stephan's heart will be filled with joy when he thinks of him.

He will never feel alone.

A celestial phenomenon he will never forget.

Stephan is at peace and full of joy.

9PM will be an hour he will forever remember.

THE SULTRY TEMPTRESS

She had a beautiful, glorious crown of dark brunette hair.

Dark wide oval eyes with long dark eyelashes which were inviting.

Her eyebrows were perfectly groomed.

A perfect arch as if painted by Leonardo da Vinci himself.

She walked liked Sophia Loren, the young Italian actress during her heyday in the classic age of Hollywood.

She was alluring and captivating.

A tigress.

A Sultry Temptress.

All eyes were on her when she walked on the streets or entered a party.

Men and women admired her, infatuation and lust.

Not only was she gorgeous, she was friendly with everyone she encountered.

You would think she was conceited, but she was not.

Her dresses fit her perfectly and tastefully.

She had a small cinched waist.

The dresses she favored were flared at the bottom, just below the knee.

She was single by choice as she wanted to meet a man that loved her not just by her looks, but, by her intellect and the love she had to give.

He didn't have to be a "Prince", just a sincere, loving and monogamous man.

A man that would want to have children as she wanted to build a family.

Swept away, yes, that's what she wanted in a man.

Sincere words from a man that was interested in a long lasting marriage, a beautiful relationship.

She often wondered if that wish would be granted in her lifetime.

Of course, it would.

It would happen at the right moment.

She had a lot to give and open to love.

He's right around the corner.

SUMMER CELEBRATION

He was very excited to attend the summer anniversary celebration being held tomorrow.

So thrilled, he only slept a few hours, looking forward to the next day ahead.

He woke up early, picked out the attire for the intimate social event as it would be a hot sultry summer day.

His goddaughter who would accompany him to the afternoon get-together, called him early in the morning to confirm the time to depart into the neighboring state.

"Padrino, I will pick you up by 1pm", she said.

Feeling full of joy, he shaved and took a long time showering to be squeaky fresh as usual.

The people he would see today, he hadn't seen in quite some time.

It's a wonderful feeling to look forward to seeing beautiful people of kind hearts and charming personalities at social events.

He wasn't sure what to bring as there would be plenty of delicious food and drink at the event.

Flowers!

Who doesn't like beautiful colored scented flowers?

Yes, the flowers would be a gift to the host of the delightful afternoon event and perhaps be used as a table centerpiece.

Along with his goddaughter, he visited the flower shop and the welcoming florists that knew him well, created a beautiful colorful bouquet of flowers.

The bouquet was tied with a beautiful red satin ribbon.

As he and his goddaughter left the florist store, the skies appeared to be menacing, dark clouds announcing a summer thunderstorm.

They paid it no mind and did not carry umbrellas.

They crossed the street and went into a NYC delicatessen to buy bottled water for their one-hour drive.

Yes, one must maintain yourself hydrated during the hot summer.

As they were about to leave the deli, the skies opened!

There was a blast of thunder, eerie lightning and it was raining "cats and dogs".

No worries.

They remained in the store until the rain calmed a bit.

Their plan was to make a run for it back to the car which was parked a couple of blocks away.

They got soaked in the rain, he admitted, it was a bit refreshing.

The rain cooled the temperatures in the environment.

Once in the car, soaking wet, the air conditioner was put on and they breathed a sigh of relief.

It was almost comical.

Fortunately, the car was new, and the a/c was functional and within a few minutes, their clothes were dry, although a bit wrinkled.

From Brooklyn, New York to Northern New Jersey.

The GPS calculated approximately a one-hour drive.

Plenty of time to get to the celebration on time.

They arrived in the beautiful State of New Jersey (USA!) a bit early and decided not to be the "early birds" at the event.

Driving to a nearby mall, they walked into a well-known chain coffee shop, to get a light bite to eat and have some coffee.

It was great for both godfather and goddaughter to spend quality time.

Talking about life, joking, and things we should not take too seriously to enjoy life.

The small meal and hot coffee for him and iced coffee for her, was satisfying, just enough.

In the shop, the godfather noticed a mother and young adolescent girl.

They were looking at the signs of the items sold in the store.

Ice cream!

He noticed the young girl pointing to a sign, depicting an ice cream sundae.

Three scoops of ice cream; vanilla, chocolate and strawberry with a peeled banana.

It was called a butterscotch sundae, like his childhood, where they were called banana boats.

He was so pleased this young girl wanted to try something different other than an ice cream cone.

The mother asked her if she wanted to try the banana boat with butterscotch topping.

She said yes to her mother.

The mother asked her if she would share the treat with her.

The young girl smiled amorously looked at her Mom and said, yes.

A happy day for them as well.

Fast forward.

He and his goddaughter drove to their destination in New Jersey.

There were several cars parked in the driveway of the house and just outside the house.

This was going to be some great shindig!

The host was his Spiritual Teacher and Mentor.

His mentor in all good things of spirituality.

When the Spiritual Teacher saw them, he smiled and greeted them so graciously and warmly.

They felt at home.

He led them to the beautiful spiritual shrine to pay their respects and homage.

He very much appreciated the flowers that they brought to him to place by his shrine.

Such peace he and his goddaughter felt.

It was not only peace, also love.

A feeling that made their hearts swell with love and gratitude.

An honor to be standing before the shrine.

As they respectfully left the shrine,

the Godfather saw so many familiar faces he had not seen in quite a while.

They greeted each other with hugs and kisses on the cheek.

Although it was awhile since he'd seen this beautiful extended family in spirituality,

it was like they had seen each other the day before and continued where they left off.

They also saw some new faces at the gathering.

They were also friendly, humble and spiritual.

His Spiritual Teacher's lovely wife's mother cooked an abundance of delicious food.

Savory stewed chicken, aromatic yellow rice with green pigeon beans also known as gandules verdes in Spanish.

Baked pork shoulder that was so tender, seasoned with garlic, pepper and spices which gave it that extra delectable flavor.

There was also boiled cassava dressed in perfectly cooked Bermuda onions that were translucent.

It was a beautiful day, and picnic tables were assembled in the backyard.

All present intermingled, spoke about spirituality and joked and laughed.

The children present were having a ball.

Some were playing badminton, while others were jumping freely on a trampoline.

The laughter of children is so refreshing and can only bring a smile to one's face.

It was great for him to sit down with his Spiritual Teacher and talk about anything.

From spirituality, politics, their favorite tv programs and lives in general.

He always enjoys his company.

He's charming, has a great sense of humor and very wise.

Everyone at the gathering had a special type of charm which exuded from their very pores.

A strong yet benevolent energy was felt all around.

Both he and his goddaughter had a great time, surrounded by a wonderful ambiance.

The sun was blazing, but that did not keep them from having fun.

He admits, he moved over to the picnic tables with the umbrellas to keep cool.

Many of the people that attended were dressed in summer whites, or bright summer colors.

It was perfect.

Both he and his goddaughter visited for a few hours, then it was time to return to New York City.

They bade their goodbyes to all with hugs and kisses once again.

Some guests were wandering through the immense beautiful backyard and they waved at them goodbye.

As they approached the car, the sun was still beaming yet from afar, they saw dark clouds.

Yikes, they both said as they laughed.

On the highway, once again a summer thunderstorm approached, and it rain heavily.

They saw a lightning strike, and both quickly looked at each other in awe of Mother Nature.

It rained heavily for about five minutes and then it subsided.

They let out a sigh of relief.

His goddaughter, sweet as always, dropped him off in front of his home.

He thanked her for the company and beautiful day they spent together and with others.

Kissed her on her cheek and gave his blessings wishing her a safe trip back to her home.

It was a beautiful afternoon spent with wonderful people.

By the way, his Spiritual Teacher and Mentor is his Godfather as well.

It was a splendid afternoon!

He looks forward to the next gathering.

THE BOY THAT HUMMED

Elijah was an adorable young boy.

He was six years old with a beautiful olive complexion and dark brown eyes.

His eyes and gaze were that of an old soul.

He was a beautiful site to see.

His parent's Noah and Isabella were beautiful too.

Noah had wavy blonde hair with green eyes and Isabella, dark brown hair and dark brown eyes.

Elijah had the looks of his exotic looking mother.

Prior to his birth, Noah and Isabella had a fairy tale marriage.

They travelled the world and had promising careers.

They both were fortunate to have genes from beautiful parents.

All eyes were on them when they walked in public holding hands affectionately.

A charming beautiful couple indeed.

They decided to wait a few years before deciding to have children.

Noah was a certified public accountant with one of the big three accounting firms and Isabella was a multilingual translator at a renown international bank.

When Noah was born, they adoringly gave all the attention they could to him.

The couple took him along on vacations.

This young boy saw parts of the world and experienced that many people have not.

Nationally within the United States; Europe, the United Kingdom and African countries.

Amusement parks, playgrounds and extracurricular activities.

Noah and Isabella gave the world to him for his young eyes to see and experience.

Elijah attended the best pre-k and after school programs in New York, excelling in all he was assigned.

He was sponge when it came to education, he absorbed it all.

Many parents observed and maliciously commented that Elijah did not resemble his father very much.

This came to the attention of Noah via gossip.

As a result, whether rational or not, made him wonder whether Elijah was his legitimate child.

Mind you, Isabella loved Noah and were always faithful.

Gossip can be vicious usually due to envy.

One day, Noah decided to have a sit down conversation with Isabella at home.

He spoke the unspeakable.

He asked her if she was ever unfaithful to him.

Isabella got emotional and cried.

How dare he ask such a question.

She loved Noah with all her heart and wouldn't fathom such an act.

It took several minutes to compose herself.

Isabella screamed at her husband for daring to ask her if she was loyal to him and the sanctity of marriage.

Enraged, she told him no!

That if he ever had any doubts, she would have their child undergo a DNA test.

Noah started to cry and shared the gossip that was being spread around.

He asked her for forgiveness for ever doubting her loyalty.

Little did they know, Elijah overheard the screaming, crying and what was discussed from his bedroom.

The young boy's reaction was to run out of his bedroom and innocently confront his parents.

Are you my daddy, asked Elijah?

Both parents hugged him and told him that everything was fine.

With tears in his eyes, Noah and Isabella him took him to his bedroom to lie him to sleep.

Elijah closed his eyes and feigned sleep.

When both parents left the room.

Elijah started to cry.

He hummed his one of his favorite songs, "Three Blind Mice.".

Elijah repeatedly hummed until he fell asleep.

This was an episode in life he would never forget.

The humming continued throughout his life when going to bed.

The boy that hummed.

Humming was his comfort when going to bed.

That one night episode marked his life.

"Three Blind Mice"

The boy that hummed.

THE CAREGIVER

She's fatigued.

Tired.

Mentally and physically exhausted.

As much she wants to give excellent care to her parent,

she is extremely overwhelmed.

She is unable to give the excellent treatment her parent deserves as she has her own health issues.

Health issues that she suffers and does not have the time to address as she needs to take care of the parent.

Crazy, huh?

One ill caregiver trying to take care of a parent that needs one hundred percent care.

The parent has dementia.

Constantly calling her daughter which is her caregiver.

Not remembering that the questions and requests are repetitive.

Emphasizing constantly.

The caregiver is tired and not seeing any light at the end of the tunnel.

The caregiver needs help herself.

Missing medical appointments, not socializing with friends and family, not leaving the home.

Reclusive.

A hermit.

Not resting, sleeping or eating adequately due to the priority given to the parent.

It's not the parent's fault.

Dementia is progressive and no cure in sight.

The parent at times has moments of lucidity, but only temporary.

The parent loves her child and vice versa, this is undeniable.

Love is and will always be present.

The caregiver pleads for help from medical professionals and encounters red tape.

No solution in sight.

She has contemplated rehabilitative and nursing home care for her parent.

Yet, the guilt of doing the latter does not permit her to do so.

Her culture has been imbedded in her mind, that family and parents are taken of at home, regardless of circumstances.

May one day soon, the right decision be made, benefiting both caregiver and parent.

THE CURSED BOY

Vito and Christine met out of the blue at a local street festival, a circus.

Once they looked at each other's eyes, it was love at first sight.

They were near an ice cream truck and struck up a conversation.

Both were single and beautiful. They could not keep their eyes off each other.

Vito was a member of a gypsy Romanian tribe, Christine a devout catholic.

Different backgrounds, yet they had something in common that could not be described.

They easily commenced a conversation by the ice cream bar and had so much in common.

Because of their different backgrounds, both were unsure if a potential relationship would work out.

Yet, they exchanged telephone numbers and kept in contact in secret.

Eventually, Vito's mother found out about their encounter and their newborn love for each other.

Vito's mother was name Carmela.

She was a fortune teller and in her tribe was known to deal with powerful black magic.

One day, Vito spoke to his mother about Christine.

His mother was furious as she was old school and only believed that gypsies only belonged with each other.

There were no interracial relationships allowed.

Vito, in love with Christine, did not care.

He wanted to be with her and build a loving life.

Christine's parents were fond of Vito and his kindness and admiration for their daughter, they were not old school.

After dating for quite some while, Vito asked Christine's family for her hand in marriage.

Christine's parents were of accord and said yes.

Due to the troublesome issues encountered, Christine and Vito married without his mother's knowledge.

As Vito's mother was a powerful clairvoyant, she knew of the secret marriage.

She was outraged and so was her tribe.

Without remorse, she swore and cursed the secret marriage.

She stated that the newly wedded couple would not bear children.

The divine intervened, and they bore a beautiful son, named Adrian.

He was heavenly.

Curly dark hair, a light olive complexion and green eyes.

A beautiful, smiling and friendly child.

Due to the evil curse put upon him by his paternal grandmother, he suffered from strange ailments.

Rashes on his body and respiratory ailments that a child of his age should not encounter.

Within three months, Adrian was christened by a compassionate pastor at the Church named Our Lady of the Snows.

When the holy water touched Adrian's head, he slowly but surely regained his health.

It was a miracle.

Through the grapevine, Carmela heard of the baptism and once again, was furious.

She attempted to curse the young boy again, but to no avail.

Adrian was protected by the most Divine.

A couple of years passed by and Carmela, wanted to meet her grandson she heard so much about.

When she met him, she was full of remorse of her wrongdoing and fell in love with him.

Adrian was an angel and adorable.

He smiled at his paternal grandmother and her heart melted.

She blessed him as well.

Good overcomes evil, sooner or later.

Love conquers hate and ignorance.

Carmela forgave her son and intertwined with the new family unit.

The Divine in all his and her manifestations resolved the hate and replaced it with love.

Adrian has grown up and is full of blessings.

God in all his and her manifestations allowed goodness to be victorious.

God bless this beautiful marriage, only son and both families.

THE DOLLS

Her mother is a doll, figuratively.

Full of happiness amongst her inanimate friends.

Dolls are so entertaining to her mother.

So entertaining, that at times, she speaks to them as if they are alive.

She interacts with them as if they were beautiful live children.

The daughter has caught her mother off-guard, having lively conversations with these beautiful creatures.

The common denominator of these dolls is that they are babies or toddlers.

One specific doll is vintage, made of porcelain with rosy cheeks and two small teeth.

A toddler, appearing to be less than two years old.

That is one of her favorites.

The mother named her Haydee.

Then there are the twin newborn babies which she also adores.

She spoils them and covers them with a small doll baby blanket.

She tells them to hush and fall asleep.

Another doll is also an infant.

An infant that shuts her eyes when laying down and eyes wide open when position to sit up.

This infant has a pacifier which makes her so adorable.

This interactive behavior makes the daughter think what her mother's childhood was like.

Perhaps she didn't have many dolls as a child?

Perhaps the interaction is a way of filling loneliness as she is a senior.

Unfortunately, not too many children, caregivers interact with the elderly.

The interaction with the dolls replaces that much needed attention by the senior lady.

It's lovely to see the senior talk to her treasured dolls, when she is alone.

The lady at times, does not care if others are watching or not, when she gives affection to the inanimate dolls.

Those are her babies, her treasured babies.

As much as the daughter wants to give all her loving attention to her mother, at times it is not possible due to other responsibilities.

The mother once told her daughter, that the day God calls upon her, to please place dolls beside her before she is laid to rest.

It may sound morbid, but it's not.

It's one of her last wishes that cannot be denied.

The lady has been a great, nourishing, caring mother during her life and the daughter appreciates it with fond memories.

The daughter wishes that her mother didn't feel so lonely.

Aging without close friends or loved ones is sad.

The daughter is happy that her mother is ecstatically happy with her baby dolls.

They keep her company; she takes care of them and offers them love and affection.

These special dolls bring laughter to her and a big smile.

May we all have that vivid imagination during the golden years of our life.

May we all have that special doll in later life, that brings us joy and makes us smile.

THE FAIRY TALE PRINCE

A very handsome man,

with the charming gift of gab.

He is financially well off, offering the world to the would-be princess.

Although not in true love, the beautiful, intelligent and articulate young

lady,

was courted in such a charming manner, that she decided to give it a

try.

She was independent with a highly visible promising career.

A career where she was more than capable to reach the stars.

He offered a glass slipper to make her his princess.

He promised her the world.

A mansion with all the furnishings and amenities that any young lady

would love.

She did not need any of this, she just wanted love.

A man to love, admire and respect her.

He was good at disguising the ugly frog he hid underneath his facade.

Promising her the world and the love she so desired.

She left all behind as she thought she found her prince charming.

It turns out that he had no real friends and no social skills.

Those that attempted to be his friends, realized that he was egotistic and thought only of himself.

Deep down inside, he wanted a beautiful trophy wife, not necessarily a princess.

He gave the glass slipper and although to the naked eye some could not see, it was tainted.

It was not the right size.

The monogamy he promised was false.

He only wanted company as he had no real friends.

Eventually, the mask he wore fell into a million pieces, bit by bit.

The disguise he wore, little by little fell apart.

The real person he hid, was finally revealed.

Fortunately, the real life princess discovered the real person behind the mask.

In time, she accepted that she did not love him, no matter how much she tried.

Jewelry, fancy clothes and other riches he offered were not enough.

She wanted a loving relationship.

He was unable to offer that.

She realized that her self esteem and love for self was much more important.

She had to move on and seek real, palpable happiness.

It took tremendous courage and sought out her happiness and love of life.

She looked deep inside herself and realized that she must seek happiness that would fulfil her.

She did.

Now she lives a life with great promise and wonderful opportunities.

Happiness and independence is in her hands now.

Bravo for her.

She is living life as should be, once again.

THE LAMP'S SECRET

I secretly love my job.

The functions of what I do are not necessarily apparent to all that see me.

I can illuminate entire rooms in a home or public domain.

The streets, buses, subways, ferries and an array of places far too many to mention.

As you sit, stand or walk by, I can hear your conversations with others.

The expressions on your face are visible to me.

In your sadness and happiness, I perceive everything if I am switched on.

I'm also present in your technological devices that require light, I sense the tapping of numbers and letters and decipher what you are writing.

In silence, I laugh and cry with you.

I'm special, perhaps different, aren't I?

Who knew that I can do all the above and more?

You cannot escape me as light is always needed in various manners.

During day or night, I am right there with you.

If you need me, just press the "ON" button or switch, and I'll be there.

THE MONSTER

It was an era then and continues to be an era now.

The Monster.

Monster is the term used by Spanish speaking people (El Monstruo), to describe the terrible disease.

El Monstruo.

The disease that many believe started in the 1980's and continues to affect all.

Scientists believe that this horrible disease goes back into earlier history, but there was no name to coin it.

It does not discriminate against men, women, children, and the LGBTQ community.

It caught everyone by surprise.

Aside from those infected by this disease, it affected their family members and friends.

No one knew how the disease would spread, therefore, causing fear.

Pneumocystis Pneumonia

Hemophilia.

Unscreened blood transfusions.

Kaposi Sarcoma.

Thrush.

The only medication that was used in the 1980's to stay alive, even for a several months,

was toxic.

AZT.

Azidothymidine.

Although AZT helped with the symptoms of infection and disease,

it was toxic.

This disease was named the gay plague.

A disease that God used to attack the "sinful", churches ostracized these folks.

The Church and other religious groups unjustly looked down on the infirmed.

The general public did not care as they were not members of the LGBTQ community.

Little did the people know, that this awful infection and disease would affect the entire world.

The entire world.

The ones that cared for the ill were physicians, scientists, nurses and those in the medical field.

The latter were also afraid as they did not know if they could be infected as well by treating these patients.

Unsafe sex.

Heroine.

Dirty needles used by heroin users.

People refrained, frightened, ashamed for various reasons to utter the name of this disease.

Here it is.

HIV.

Human immunodeficiency Virus.

Ultimately, HIV untreated or treated, eventually became the dreaded disease.

AIDS.

Acquired Immune Deficiency Syndrome.

Sadly, family members and friends, perhaps due to fear, disassociated themselves from those affected by El Monstruo.

Many people died at a very early age; innocent children, teens, 20's, 30's, the elderly, those that had a whole life ahead of them.

Discrimination was rampant.

The infected were afraid to tell their friends, family and their employers as to not lose their relationships and jobs.

Now, in the present, fortunately, there are medications that control HIV and its progression to AIDS.

Yet, AIDS still affect many and those same medications lengthen human lives.

Humans.

Human lives.

Many still do not find it comfortable to discuss this disease.

They are afraid and ashamed.

They have family members that have this disease and will not utter a word to anyone about them.

There have been cases of two men who were HIV positive with other immunological disease and bone marrow transplants were used.

It apparently, "cured" them of AIDS.

This is still being studied and a dangerous procedure.

The scientific community has been diligently working on finding a cure.

No real cure in sight.

May that day come soon.

THE PINK SLEEPING GOWN

The sleeping gown, which is short in length, is a beautiful pink.

A faded rose color.

Pamela owned this gown for many years, but had it stored away in her dresser draw.

Typically, her sleep wear was pant pajama sets.

When summer came around, she decided to wear the pink sleeping gown.

It was refreshing.

Sleeveless, made of Egyptian cotton.

Very comfortable.

The neckline and the surround area of the short tank top sleeves were laced beautifully, also made of soft white cotton.

It had a delicate and very feminine look.

When Pamela wore it, she was in heaven, very comfortable.

If it got too cool in her room, she covered herself with a summer lavender colored sheet.

Very pleasant feeling as well.

When company was not present, she would sit on the edge of the bed to ponder.

She allowed her mind to go with the flow of thoughts.

At times, talking to herself.

She was always reminiscing about her past and what the future held for her.

Pamela at times was lost in her thoughts.

She is in her golden years, a beautiful senior.

She is of a fair skin tone and had good genetics, thanks to her ancestors.

A smooth face and very pretty.

What does she think about when she sits on the edge of her bed?

She smiles and thinks about all the adventures in her life.

The turmoil's and triumphs she experienced.

It's fascinating, that a piece of clothing affects the mind and body.

Perhaps she wonders when her calling to the heavens will come.

It's evident that she feels lonely.

Her caregivers observe the aforementioned.

Although they are by her side physically, sadness and loneliness seeps into her mind and soul.

Her comfort for now, is the pink sleeping gown.

The gown brings her back to the times of happiness.

Colors are magical.

The pretty pink color was made perfectly for her.

"THE SHOWER"

Taking a shower should be so easy.

Soothing, in and out.

Yet, the act of taking a shower for her was a challenge.

She loved showering, yet, focusing made it difficult.

She used a sponger with a deliciously scented body wash.

Everything had to be planned out before entering the shower.

Although not professionally diagnosed with obsessive compulsive disorder (OCD),

she appeared to manifest those symptoms.

Turning on the hot water first, to heat the bathroom during winter.

Adjusting the cold water along with hot to make it comfortable.

Washing her hair first, was the first task, twice.

Applying the hair conditioner to last 3 minutes on her beautiful hair.

Quickly after that, pouring some of the bath wash on the sponge.

Focusing to clean parts of her body first and rinse in a specific order.

Left arm first, washing off with water, followed by the right arm.

Washing her chest and back of body with the foaming sponge and rinsing off once again.

All had to be in meticulously in order.

Private parts are washed repeatedly.

Left leg and foot followed by the right leg and foot.

Ensuring that she washed carefully between the toes and the soles of her feet.

At times forgetting whether she covered all body parts.

If she was unsure, she would repeat the same washing routine.

Drying her body with the 100 percent cotton towel, part by part in a specific order.

Finally, stepping out of the shower and ensuring she dried every part of her body.

For the majority, showering is easy.

Unfortunately, it was not for her.

Showering was quite a challenge.

Oh, can't forget the face, same challenge.

Eventually, she will overcome this alarming response of just showering.

A psychological issue.

Someday, she will acknowledge this problem and seek help.

THE SIREN AND MERMAN

The Siren and Merman were thought to be mythological creatures.

The Siren also called Mermaids, were composed of an upper body of a beautiful woman, and the lower body of a fish with a wide strong tail to swiftly swim underneath the seas.

The Merman was her counterpart, half human male and with attributes of the fish lower body.

Such beautiful creatures.

Both donned long, beautiful hair neatly groomed with brushes made of sea coral.

They lived in a kingdom deep in the ocean, undetected by mankind for millennia.

There was the King and Queen which reigned over this colorful cold domain.

They lack nothing.

The mermaids were known to peek above the ocean and see the human seamen, at times making themselves visible to them.

The sirens would sing in such beautiful voices, their mode of communication.

The seaman became enchanted.

They jumped in the waters, to be near them.

The mermaids did not want to hurt them, and their intentions were not to drown them.

Yet many inadvertently drowned to meet and touch these beautiful creatures.

The men who survived, lived to recount their experiences.

Mankind, did not believe them, scoffing at them and stated that they were insane.

But all was true, there novels were written of these encounters between humans and mermaids.

Whether one believed the "novel" which were more like autobiographies, people were entranced.

Were the real or just imaginary?

The authors of these books were wholeheartedly convinced that it was real.

These creatures lived underneath the seas for millennia without aging.

There was something in the waters, which was dew of youth.

Magical.

Unbeknownst to mankind, they had the ability to walk undetected amongst humans on earth to know about their whereabouts.

They were saddened to see how the humans destroyed the ocean and earth.

This was reported to the King and Queen that lived in the depths of the sea.

As much, as these water creatures want to help mankind, they could not.

They allowed nature to take its place, allowing the humans to reap what they sowed.

Eventually, some of the humans would be enlightened and see the damage the instilled upon plant Earth and tried to correct it.

There were many tales, of which humans tried to capture these creatures in fishing nets during their exploration of the unknown, the depths of the ocean.

They were unable to, as the strength of the mermaids and merman was beyond the human abilities.

They escaped and skimmed back into the depths of the seas.

Fantasy?

No, it was true.

These adventures were captured in old and new texts by the humans.

Those who read them, thought them to be insane.

But the authors, new the truth.

The navigators could never reach the kingdom as it was infinitely hidden from human eyes.

The sirens and merman continue to live, undisturbed in this beautiful kingdom.

Filled with creatures with an intellect that is incalculable.

A beauty that escapes the human vocabulary.

Beware.

These creatures may appear at night and capture your imagination, making you jump into the cold waters.

See them from afar and let them be.

Never speak of them as your will be deemed insane.

You don't want that, right?

Keep those memories to yourself and be honored to have witnessed such an experience.

Do the beautiful mermaids and merman exist?

Yes.

No one knows what lays at the depths of the sea.

Do not ask me how I know, I just do.

TOUGH TIMES

He observed, that folks are experiencing tough times financially.

For a certain class of people to survive, he noticed,

they had to find other resources to pay their bills, groceries and

everyday necessities.

Yes, necessity, not luxury.

A mode of survival in life.

He saw people in the streets all over the parts of the city,

doing all they can do, to collect a nickel, a dime, quarter, and if

fortunate enough a few dollars.

These folks come from all different backgrounds.

Many are employed but are living from check to check.

Some have second jobs to make ends meet.

Decent people.

He saw folks of all races, going to neighborhoods where they would not be recognized to make those ends meet.

Collecting recyclable beverage bottles and cans, from garbage cans in the street.

Trash bins labeled "Recycle" for the city sanitation to collect.

They carried clear plastic garbage bags placed in food shopping carts or just in their hands.

Going from place to place, house to house, luxury skyscrapers to find these valuable recycling products.

During the summer, they covered their heads to avoid heat exhaustion, during the winter, hats and gloves to maintain their hands warm.

He's come across these people and although a bit embarrassed they nodded their heads and smiled.

America, the land of opportunity.

Not all had great opportunities, nonetheless, they astutely found this form of making money.

Making ends meet.

On a good day, these clear plastic bags were full of recyclables and the collectors were more than grateful.

Carrying these bags in carts or on their weary backs.

Bringing these recyclables to convenience stores to cash them in.

This much needed monetary currency was for food to feed themselves, friends and family.

These were long days spent in the street, during unbearable heat, pouring rain, snow and all elements of nature.

No one in their home neighborhood needed to know.

They returned with the bags hidden in their backpacks or purses, neatly folded.

Only those that needed to know, knew of their escapades.

Tomorrow would be another day for them.

Their hope was to find these recyclables available to survive tough times.

Each can, each plastic bottle was a blessing.

A nickel, a dime, quarter and perhaps a dollar in total.

Grateful for these blessings.

It was their contribution to their families.

May the Divine bless them always.

If you enjoyed reading this book, please see other works by the author, available for purchase on Amazon.

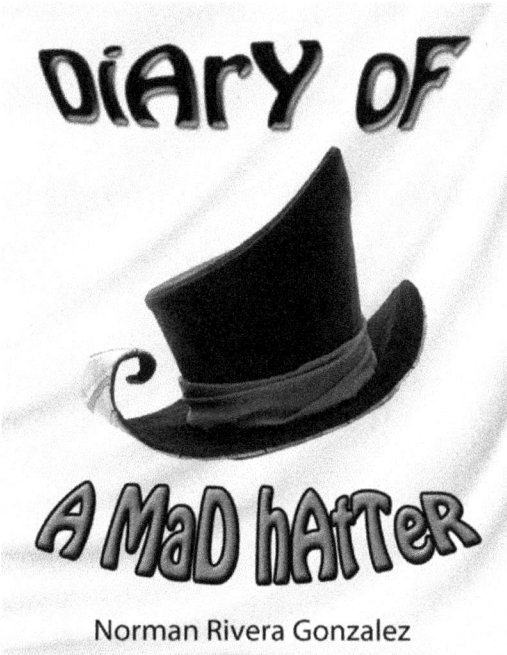

DiARY OF

A MaD hATTeR

Norman Rivera Gonzalez

Darkness And Lightness
Observations,
Moments of Dark and Light
We All Experience

By Norman Rivera Gonzalez

mpliance